TOO PRECIOUS
TO LOSE

A young Jason G. Green perched on his
grandmother's shoulder

TOO
PRECIOUS
TO LOSE

*A Memoir of Family,
Community, and Possibility*

JASON G. GREEN

ONE WORLD
NEW YORK

One World
An imprint of Random House
A division of Penguin Random House LLC
1745 Broadway, New York, NY 10019
oneworldlit.com
penguinrandomhouse.com

Hardcover ISBN 978-0-593-73171-0
Ebook ISBN 978-0-593-73172-7

Printed in the United States of America

1st Printing

First Edition

BOOK TEAM: Production editor: Luke Epplin • Managing editor: Rebecca
Berlant • Production manager: Mark Maguire • Copy editor: Julie Ehlers •
Proofreaders: Martin Schneider, Kate Hertzog, Claire Maby

Book design by Susan Turner

The authorized representative in the EU for product safety and compliance
is Penguin Random House Ireland, Morrison Chambers, 32 Nassau Street,
Dublin D02 YH68, Ireland. https://eu-contact.penguin.ie

For My Family

The Pleasant View Methodist Episcopal Church

Precious mem'ries, how they linger,
How they ever flood my soul;
In the stillness of the midnight,
Precious, sacred scenes unfold.

—J.B.F. WRIGHT and LONNIE B. COMBS,
   "Precious Memories"

CONTENTS

The original Quince Orchard Colored School building,
with students outside

AUTHOR'S NOTE

I N 1967, DR. KING, IN HIS FINAL BOOK, ASKED: *WHERE DO WE go from here? Chaos or community?*

For the longest time, I assumed the answer was obvious—community. We would choose one another. We would build and progress together. That was what I was taught and grew up believing.

But now I understand why Dr. King posed his prophetic question, and I worry.

I worry about the rising tide of racial and political animus and how easily it turns us inward—and on each other.

I worry about a future rushing toward us, widening a gulf between the haves and the have-nots.

I worry that profit eclipses humanity, dignity, and respect.

I worry because it matters how we see each other, and that we see each other.

I worry because choosing community isn't as obvious as I

once, perhaps naïvely, believed. Alas, almost sixty years later, most signs still point to chaos.

I get it. Chaos is faster. Louder. It gets more clicks. Community moves slowly. It demands more of us and requires grace and intention.

This book is about that kind of work. The kind that makes us slow down and truly *remember*. It was unexpected to walk into a room to sit by my ailing ninety-five-year-old grandmother's side, a blessing to walk out forever changed.

I wrote this book as an enduring reminder that our collective yesterdays, no matter how troubled, light our path toward better tomorrows.

I choose community because some things are too precious to lose.

—Jason G. Green

PROLOGUE

OUR PEDIATRICIAN'S OFFICE BUZZED WITH ENERGY DE-spite it being 6:45 A.M. I bounced our six-month-old son gently in my arms as my wife, Ritu, and I waited. Behind the reception desk, a nurse hurriedly typed his information into the system amid ringing phones and caffeinating staff.

"His name is Aidan. Two A's." I raised my voice above the commotion. Since his birth in October 2024, I'd become unexpectedly protective of his name, correcting anyone who misspelled it with an insistence that surprised even me.

While we waited, I studied the wall of patient photos, a rainbow of innocent, smiling young faces representing children of every racial hue. It sparked an idea for Pleasant View, my family's home church, with deep historic roots. Perhaps we could do something similar to honor all those who had joined Pleasant View's restoration effort and hang a picture of everyone who had raised a hammer, donated a dollar, or gotten their hands dirty in that Quince Orchard soil. All those different people were breathing life back into structures that had stood as symbols of community for more than a century.

Growing up in the 1980s and '90s, living through our Maryland community's shift from rural to suburban, I didn't have to wonder about the possibility of integration. I inherited it. I was born into a congregation whose enduring legacy was the fight for racial equality. In many ways, Dr. Martin Luther King, Jr.'s "Beloved Community" was its origin story realized. The community intentionally worked toward it, and generations later it had quietly shaped how I saw the world.

Aidan's fidgeting snapped my attention back to him. He had just learned to roll and was putting his new talents to work. The previous six months had been a blur of diaper changes and sleepless nights. It seemed just a moment ago that my shoulder pushed against the delivery room door, my heart racing with anticipation as I awaited all the dizzying, beautiful chaos that followed—doctors' voices, my wife's determination, monitors beeping, and then, finally, the singular miracle of Aidan's first cry.

In a nation mired in division, struggling to hold on to its very identity as a democracy, the birth of my first child was both a welcome distraction and a reminder of what truly mattered. It took us a few days to pick a name. We tried to name him after my father's mother but couldn't find a derivation of "Pearl" that felt quite right. And, given the way Aidan would turn bright red when he cried, a name that means "fiery one" seemed fitting.

My grandmother taught me that truth reveals itself in layers, in whispers, in stories that circle back to the beginning just when you think you've reached the end. Like finding new meaning in a familiar place. Or discovering new symbolism in a name. I didn't understand then that sometimes the most important discoveries aren't found by merely opening new doors, but by first returning to the thresholds we've already crossed. Like Sankofa, the age-old West African philosophy that says "go back and get it," sometimes we must look back in order to map the course ahead.

My phone vibrated in my pocket. Kisha's name flashed on the screen. It was my older sister's second call that morning. Strange for this early hour. I bounced Aidan once more, but this time I answered.

"Jason," she said, her voice steady but thin. "It's Grandma. It's her foot again."

TOO PRECIOUS
TO LOSE

1

I WALKED, ALMOST GLIDED, DOWN A NARROW CORRIDOR, MY arms gently extended. I was following so closely behind myself I could almost kick my back leg to make it buckle, like we used to do playfully back in the day. Something about the barren walls and humming fluorescent glow felt familiar, but I couldn't place it. My outstretched hand skipped from the rail, floated through the gap left by a doorframe, and landed back in place. Surprised my high-top sneakers weren't squeaking against the linoleum, I looked down to investigate and came to a stop in front of a closed door.

When I looked back up, I could see a number beside the door. There was no name, just a number. I was drawn to it and could sense someone was waiting behind it. I gathered myself to knock, but before anyone could even answer, I turned the knob, leaned my shoulder into the door, and pushed it open. Just before entering the room, I craned my neck to get a peek at who was inside.

I jolted upright in bed.

Adrenaline, more than fear. I had the feeling of something unresolved.

My eyes followed the blades of the ceiling fan. It was early, around 5 A.M., and the chances of falling back to sleep seemed slim. Besides, I liked getting to work early. I pulled myself into the shower and played the usual morning game: blue or black suit? Definitely not the tan. Never the tan.

As I buttoned my shirt, the dream repeated in my head. *What was I chasing?*

After spending nearly a year and a half working on the 2008 Obama campaign, I had been swept up in the fast-moving wave of new hires flowing into President Obama's administration. During the campaign, I'd held a few different roles, including National Voter Registration Director. But now it was 2009, and at twenty-seven I was appointed to serve as one of the president's lawyers in the White House Counsel's office.

My appointment came with many spectacular things, the opportunity to do meaningful work, a coveted White House badge, brilliant colleagues, work that made me think, occasional tickets to the president's box at the Kennedy Center, an invite to play basketball on the highest court in the land, boxes of presidential M&Ms, even the clout to offer the occasional behind-the-scenes White House tour. But one thing I didn't get? An office. That's right, instead I got a bullpen—a glorified conference room that I shared with three talented young lawyers: Ian Bassin, Rashad Hussein, and Blake Roberts.

For months it didn't bother us. Until it did. And then each of us started to groan at meetings, "Any update on those offices?"

As attorneys, it could get a little awkward. A client might walk in seeking counsel. I'd say, "Tell me what's going on," and they'd glance around the wide-open space, with others listening in, and ask, "Here?"

Our bullpen was on the west side of the Old Executive Office Building lodged between the executive gym and 17th Street NW. The OEOB (or EEOB, depending on who you ask) was a hulking landmark, which had taken seventeen years to construct, that had stood beside the White House since the late 1800s. Once called the "greatest monstrosity in America," the building first housed the departments of State, War, and the Navy, but since 1939, it has served as home to White House staff.

I faced our heavy slab of mahogany (one of more than 1,300 interior doors in the building), and as my shoulder leaned to push it open, it clicked: *This must be the hallway from my dream.* I felt a little silly dreaming about office space but relieved I'd at least figured it out. I turned and hustled down the corridor, late for our team meeting.

During the early days of the Obama administration, the Office of the White House Counsel crowded into the Counsel's West Wing office for weekly all-hands meetings. This office had been established in 1943 to provide the president, vice president, and senior staff of the Executive Office of the President with legal advice informed by both constitutional and political considerations, preserving the independence of the Attorney General and Department of Justice. These meetings were usually pretty routine.

But that week we had a special guest and needed more space. To accommodate, our meeting was moved to the Situation Room.

The Situation Room is an SCIF—a sensitive compartmented information facility—meaning phones and other devices aren't allowed inside. We checked and catalogued ours at the door. Even that small ritual stirred the political nerd in me. The Situation Room had been created at President Kennedy's direction in 1961 in the wake of the Bay of Pigs Invasion, and now I was there, sliding into history.

The White House could grow routine over time, but things like the Situation Room never did. The glow of strategically positioned flat screens on every wall gives the room a high-tech feel. Intimidation was built into the design. I looked around at the command center, with its sense of consequence, and felt like I'd stepped into a political thriller where world-altering decisions unfold in hushed tones.

As we all shuffled in, I became hyperaware of my own presence and place. I was the youngest lawyer on the team. The only one who hadn't clerked for a prominent judge or worked for a big-name law firm. In fact, aside from the campaign, I hadn't worked in law at all. This was technically my first legal job after law school. That morning, I felt every bit of my little gap-toothed Black kid who'd grown up on a dirt road self.

The centerpiece of the room was an imposing conference table, surrounded by sleek, high-backed leather chairs, the highest back reserved, of course, for the president or most senior staffer. Less conspicuous seats lined the perimeter, seemingly far from the action. I backed away from the table and slid into a seat positioned on the periphery as close to the door as I could find. A few colleagues gravitated toward the table, but most, like me, were happy to take a seat along the wall.

Then President Obama walked in. He made his way to his

chair, surveying the empty seats around the table. He glanced at those of us happily perched along the walls, notebooks open for note-taking, safely removed from the center of action.

"Who are you waiting for?" he bellowed, not looking at anyone in particular, but it felt like he was talking directly to me. "Take your seat at the table. We've got work to do."

For a second, the words rattled around in my head.

Who are you waiting for?

Take your seat at the table.

We've got work to do.

The president was calling us to action. Reminding us that no one else was coming to fill those empty seats. We were the ones entrusted with the opportunities and responsibilities before us. *Yes!* I thought. *Let's go! This* was why I signed up to work for this administration. Despite all the reasons I'd convinced myself I should sit quietly, my age, my race, my background, here was the POTUS telling the first-legal-job-having me to roll up my sleeves, pull up my chair, and take my place at the table. Because I belonged there and we had work to do.

Ever since I was a kid, all I wanted was to do something, anything, that would make people's lives better. Growing up, I'd envied the friends who could articulate the exact job they wanted. That was never me. I didn't have a title in mind. I just knew I wanted my work to matter. And the White House? The White House mattered. Growing up in the D.C. region, I couldn't help but revere the building and the office it held. When I got the job in the Counsel's office, I didn't let myself show how thrilled I was. I tried to play it cool, tried to act like I belonged. In D.C., you're supposed to grumble about the traffic, the hours, the lawyers, and the bureaucracy. That's how people know you're serious. I was floating down those halls, but I made sure no one saw my feet leave the ground.

One morning, I was late for a meeting, rushing down a corridor in the West Wing. Hugging the wall coming around a tight corner, I nearly collided with Rahm Emanuel, the president's chief of staff, infamous for his steel-melting temperament and the dead fish story that had made him a legend. It was rumored he sent one to a Democratic pollster. As we brushed past each other, I heard him yell, "Goddamn lawyer!"

My only thought? *Wow! He does know who I am.* That was Washington.

It was a time of adrenaline and awe, elbows and elegance, sometimes all wrapped in the same moment. Yet, amid the mayhem, there were these rituals that reminded me why I loved being there in the first place.

Early each morning, I'd arrive at the East Wing Gate, tie tucked in my pocket. After the Secret Service checkpoint, I'd weave among the early-bird tourists lined up for their public tour. I loved blending in with them and basking in their wonder as they toured the East Wing. Sometimes I'd drop a quick White House fact as they gazed at some portrait, just to get their *oohs* and *aahs*: "Did you know that the Brady Press Room was actually built over the old pool, which is still there?"

Just past the China Room, tall vertical dividers stood like ceremonial gates, flanked by armed Secret Service officers. They marked the edge of the public tour. Guests were ushered up the stairs to the main ceremonial floors. But with the right badge, you could slip between the dividers, to the surprise of those looking on from the public tour groups, and disappear into the belly of the beast toward the West Wing.

My portfolio in the Counsel's office was broad. One day I'd help weigh deep constitutional questions about executive privilege, the next, I'd help determine whether birthday cupcakes in the Roosevelt Room required ethics clearance. One of the more obscure components of my portfolio was overseeing the use of the image and likeness of the president, the presidential seal, the White House, and the first family. I got the portfolio because frankly Karen Dunn told me I had to take it, no one else really wanted it, and I was too junior to say no. But I came to love it. I became a guardian of the first family's likeness. For example, if you ever got a letter denying your request to put Michelle Obama's face on a T-shirt—sorry, that was probably me.

That work deepened my reverence for the institution. Few others were around at that early hour, and the stillness made the place feel even more special. I cherished my walk, dodging the porters as they vacuumed and prepared the building for the day: through the Palm Room, tracing the West Colonnade, drifting past the Rose Garden and the Cabinet Room, breezing by the Roosevelt Room, then heading down the stairs, out the door, across the West Executive parking lot, and back up the Navy Stairs into the Old Executive Office Building. It was no shortcut. But it was worth it.

Even on the toughest day, that morning routine grounded me. There was something magical about the energy of the tourists juxtaposed against the stillness of watching the building wake up. Even when Bo, the Obamas' Portuguese Water Dog, barked at me like I was trespassing, it all felt like a secret just for me.

And in the evening, I'd walk out the North Gate and the

portico would be illuminated, and some tourist would inevitably ask:

"Excuse me, sir, do you work there?"

Looking back over my shoulder at the building in its evening glory, I'd confirm, "I do."

"Wow. What's it like to work for the president?"

"There's nothing better than serving the American people." I never said it for effect—I meant it every time.

But even then, I was starting to wonder what else I might be missing.

Then I'd loosen my tie and hustle unceremoniously across Lafayette Square to catch the S4 bus heading north up 16th Street.

2

M Y BLUE NOKIA HANDHELD BUZZED.

It was my mom.

I was on a deadline for a memo, so I let it go to voicemail.

A moment later my desk phone rang. Mom again.

She never called that number. In fact, I wasn't sure she had that number, which meant she had looked up the White House switchboard, called, and had them transfer her. Something was up.

I snatched the desk phone before it went to voicemail.

"Jason."

The quiver in my mother's voice betrayed the calm she was trying to convey. I knew Grandma Green had not been doing well. Grandma Green is my father's mother, but over the years she and my mother had grown just as close. Grandma was ninety-five years old and a hard patient to read. We could never really tell how she was doing because she viewed the world with evergreen optimism and never let on about her troubles. Despite her being born Black in 1918 and educated and employed throughout the segregated Jim Crow years, if I were to ask Grandma the hardest thing she'd ever been through, she would say something like, "Well, if you believe in God, and work hard, everything will work out just fine."

"The doctors say . . ." Mom paused, collecting herself. "They say her circulation is failing. They're recommending she amputate her leg, but she has refused. At ninety-five, that means . . ."

She didn't finish the sentence. She didn't need to.

I sat frozen. The memo open in front of me didn't matter anymore. I thought about each Sunday dinner I'd missed, every breakfast conversation I hadn't made time for, all of the questions I hadn't asked Grandma. The woman who had shown up for literally every milestone in my life was slipping away. And I'd been too busy to notice.

I grew up close to my grandparents. Close to the rest of my family, too. Sometimes too close.

I'm descended from a rural community situated about thirty miles northwest of the nation's capital. So is my grandma. When she came up in the 1920s, and even in the 1950s when my father was coming up, the community was known as Quince Orchard. Over time it has gone by different names, but growing up it was Gaithersburg to me.

I was raised on fellowship—the place and the principle. My two sisters and I spent our childhood on Fellowship Lane, a quarter-mile hill with a gentle decline. Both our parents worked in the school system at different points in their careers, and my dad layered on becoming a United Methodist minister when we were quite young. Community and service were a big part of our early orientation. When I was born, our street wasn't yet called Fellowship Lane; it was just an unpaved dirt road. Still, there was a rhythm to life there.

My friends from the more paved parts of town referred to our street as the "bumpy road." It wasn't like the newer, well-manicured streets of the planned communities that were quickly encircling us. It was a vestige of an older way of life, and each time we turned onto our street it felt like we were going back in time.

The gravel lane was adorned with a tangle of dense vines. I thought our Dodge minivan might one day succumb to the botanical abyss. Ms. Talley, who amazingly was one of two un-related Anna Talleys on our street, lived at the top of the hill in a one-story pink house that welcomed you to the neighbor-hood. Her matching concrete garage was so close to the road it forced careful drivers, like my mom, to slow down. Mom would bring the van down to a crawl to keep the garage from scratch-ing the paint and to keep the deep potholes caused by snow and rainstorms from jacking up her alignment. So slowly we could feel every pothole's peak and valley. Dad, on the other hand, had all the craters memorized and could navigate the street without slowing, jerking the wheel left and right, kicking up a huge dust cloud as he eased on down the lane.

Delicious little honeysuckle blossoms sprouted out of the vines and trees. The smell still transports me right back. We didn't even have to get out of the car to reach the honeysuckle and berries just sat right outside the backseat window. We were careful, though, because Grandpa Green liked to scare us with stories about those branches: "One tore a girl's arm clear off," he'd warn. Our arms were spared but that's more than I could say for the paint on the car. We had our scrapes and bruises, but life on Fellowship was a special way to grow up. In many ways, my street was the last vestige of the Black community of Quince Orchard, which had persisted for more than a hundred years before disappearing from the map. When I was a kid, I didn't even know Quince Orchard had ever existed, but we'll get to all that.

My grandparents, Ida Pearl and Gerard Green, lived at the top of that quarter-mile hill in the little white house with green shutters where my father and his two brothers, the older from my grandmother's first marriage, and their older sister, from my grandfather's first marriage, spent their formative years. Their two-story home, which my grandfather built by hand some forty years before I came along, sat at the intersection of Quince Orchard Road and that bumpy dirt road that would become Fellowship Lane.

Dotted between my grandparents' house and my parents' were cousins, aunts, uncles, and people we called aunt, uncle, or cousin. Our community was one of those places where blood had little to do with whether you were considered family. We often ended up over at my Aunt Helen's house for cookouts and holidays, where after dinner we would play volleyball until the nets sagged. Everyone who lived on our little gravel road then was Black, but the broader community looked quite different.

Grandpa Green kept pigs and cows, and we lived next door to his farm. A small tin structure on his property housed the pigs and hosted butchering day, which was held at least once a year.

Years later, in law school, I'd silently chuckle during property law discussions about nuisance. My classmates debated hypothetical cases of living beside a pig farm while we'd lived the real thing. On butchering day, a half dozen relatives would arrive before sunup, my grandfather orchestrating the proceedings with quiet efficiency while my grandmother and aunts commanded the kitchen back at the house.

More than once, the pigs escaped their pen and made their way through the old chain-link fence that separated them from our house. My older sister, Kisha, would be perched at our back door, overlooking our small wooden deck, Paul Revereing the play-by-play of their steady ascent toward our house. *The pigs are coming! The pigs are coming!* They would trot up into the backyard past the big red barn.

That barn had its own stories. My older cousins Kevin and Tim kept their dirt bike there that they would ride up and down the lane and in between the fruit trees in the yard. Once, I tried to take it out on my own, but I was too little. It tipped and fell on top of me before I even got it started. Grandpa Green had actually built the barn to house Dolly, the pony he'd given to Kisha as a gift. Dolly was part of the family. She was sweet most days, but not without drama. My cousin Crystal once tumbled off her and broke her arm. One winter, Mom was walking down to feed her and slipped on the ice, spraining her finger.

Those winters could be brutal. Blizzards would blanket our little dirt drive, restrict any movement, and sometimes, to Kisha's and my delight, cancel school days in advance. Montgomery County refused to clear the snow on our dirt road because the road was unpaved, and, ironically, they also refused to pave the road. My grandfather's voice would rise with indignation each time he'd explain this circular logic. "They won't pave it," he'd say, pausing to spit out some of his chewing tobacco, "because Black folks live here, and then they say don't clear it 'cause it isn't paved. Don't make no sense!" Grandpa had seen too many "coincidences" in his lifetime and would make the same declaration every time a heavy snow would keep someone from getting to school or work or cut them off from the world in some other way. Disruptive snows seemed a more regular occurrence back then.

It may have been terrible for the adults, but it was kind of idyllic for us kids. At the Green house, when we got snowed in, we spent the morning walking in each other's footsteps so as not to violate the beauty of the expanse of undisturbed snow. But that didn't last long; we were anxious to sled down those hills. The best snowfalls had a layer of frozen snow on top to help support our steel-runner sled. Mom needed convincing, but not as much as you might expect, to get bundled up and on the sled. She grew up in Columbus, Ohio, after her ancestors had moved from Virginia during the Great Migration. She would proudly proclaim how her childhood winters dwarfed our measly temperatures and snowfalls.

Regardless, I was thankful for the training those winters had given her, as she was hands down the best sled navigator of the family. Respectfully, Dad was too heavy. The back of the sled would just sink into the snow as soon as he sat on it. And when I tried to drive it, I would inevitably close my eyes in fear and steer us directly into a tree, a snowdrift, or, worse, the creek bed down at the bottom of our property. We would exhaust ourselves during the day on sled run after sled run up and down the hill.

And at night, if the power was out, as it seemed to often be, we would hit up the food supply that Mom kept in the upright freezer to try to eat the frozen food before it spoiled. My favorite nights were when we would break out the tray of frozen Chinese food appetizers, not thinking it odd to make a meal out of appetizers. I know pork egg rolls are not intended to be cooked by fire, but somehow Mom could get them to just the right level of crisp. With our makeshift buffet, we would play The Game of Life by candlelight. On normal days, I could not stand The Game of Life, but somehow in those moments without distraction, I couldn't imagine doing anything else.

After a day or two of being snowed in, when people really needed to get out to get to the grocery store or back to a job (well before the days of Zoom), all the men would come together and shovel out our little neighborhood. I would wrap myself in my blue-and-black-striped robe and press myself into the bay window in the living room to watch my dad, uncles, neighbors, and older cousins shovel a little and laugh a lot. Even our neighbor Mr. Clipper, who had lost part of his foot, would be out there too, shoveling away. I longed to be old enough to go help. Eventually Aunt Esther or Ms. Talley, or whoever desperately needed out of the neighborhood, would honk jubilantly as their car would fishtail its way up the hill, freed from the temporary ice prison and jolted forward by traction from the little scraps of cardboard strategically placed along the narrow, excavated path.

Some years later, after much pleading, organizing, and hard work, the county agreed to pave our gravel lane. Rev. Talley, surprisingly of no blood relation to the owner of the concrete garage at the top of the street, lived at the bottom of the street not far from my parents. It was Rev. Talley who suggested the street be named Fellowship Lane in honor of the camaraderie in good times and bad that took place on that street. From shoveling each other out of blizzard conditions to sharing prime meats after butchering day; all the days when necessity demanded your neighbor be your insurance policy against the vicissitudes of life. And so our little lane of fellowship became Fellowship Lane.

It was the perfect name for our little street, in our little community. Even if at times it felt a little too little for me.

Ronnie Dogget, a friend from elementary school, came over to play in the yard one afternoon. It was a special occasion because I usually only got to play with church friends. I got along with everyone but couldn't quite gain full admission to the cool kids' club. I claimed it was because my parents refused to buy cool kids' clothes. I'm not sure if it was the cost or the principle, but I remember having to use a Magic Marker more than once to black out the extra stripe on my "Adidas" sneakers.

Ronnie was definitely a cool kid. He could fold his socks down so they hugged his ankles instead of drooping like mine did. And his jeans were always pegged just right. When he arrived, Dad pulled us over for a quick talk. "Do not let me find you playing in that pipe," he said, motioning toward the drainpipe recently installed down by the creek. A declaration like that serves two purposes for a child like me: 1) it put me on notice that there was a new pipe worthy of exploring, and 2) it told me to be extra careful and not let Dad find us playing in said pipe.

There was a thick patch of woods behind my parents' house. Kisha and I had explored nearly every inch of those woods, climbed about half the trees, and knew the terrain cold. I led Ronnie toward the edge of the woods, then, once Dad was back in the house, we doubled back along the tree line to where the pipe was hidden. It was huge, at least eight feet wide, and it beckoned like a siren song. I stepped into the pipe without any prompting. Ronnie followed me in to check out our forbidden playground.

It was glorious. Sound echoed beautifully through the pipe. As we yelled back and forth at each other, we could hear our words bounce off the internal walls, not fully appreciating how the sound would also carry beyond the pipe. We waddled like ducks, straddling the stream of water running through the middle to keep our shoes dry. But I lost my footing and slipped, landing on my back squarely in the muck. While my behind was still half-submerged in the water, I looked up to see a silhouette at the entrance to the pipe.

Busted.

Sunlight streamed into my eyes, and I couldn't exactly make out the figure, but I had a good idea of who it was. But when I heard "I know you're not playing in that pipe," it was worse than I'd originally thought. Grandpa Green!?! The pipe was right next to where he kept his pigs. I should have thought of that.

The only thing worse than getting caught by my father was getting caught by my grandfather and then delivered to my outraged father. Grandpa Green marched us right up the hill to our house and presented me to my father. Dad, with disappointment on his face, landed a stinging, wet smack right across my backside. I wasn't sure if he was doing it more for Grandpa or for Ronnie.

Dad called Ronnie's parents to get him, and I wondered if Dad was embarrassed that he had to make that call.

Meanwhile, I was mortified. I moped in my room, plotting my escape from Fellowship Lane, convinced I'd never be a cool kid.

Then there was also the time that Dad took me and my buddy Philip with him to the Safeway up on Darnestown Road. As Dad shopped, we meandered the aisles, posturing in front of older girls. At one point, I grabbed a blueberry muffin out of the bakery. I ate the top, then, as we were checking out, stashed the rest behind a display of *National Enquirer* magazines beyond view of my father's watchful eye.

Outside the store, just as we were getting back to the car, Dad turned to me and said, "Jason, did you pay for your muffin?"

I froze. "Uhhh. No, I thought you did." He didn't say a word. Just gave me the look. That look.

I slowly turned around and shuffled back into the Safeway, pulled the half-eaten muffin from behind the tabloids, and stepped back in line.

The checkout woman had watched me reverse my way back up her line. The whole time her eyes were scanning my face, as if she were running me against her internal facial recognition software. Before I could say, "I'd like to pay for this," she asked, "Hey, are you Pearl Green's grandson? You have her eyes." I wanted to dig a hole and bury myself in it. I nodded, and the checkout woman smiled a big smile. "I love your grandma."

I should have said something like "Thank you, I love her too." But I didn't. I just mumbled and walked off, embarrassed to be caught and even more embarrassed to be known. I'd rather she had been disappointed with me on principle than adored me by association.

And then there was the tractor.

One afternoon, our school bus got stuck in traffic. It was a rare occasion for us to be sitting in traffic. Kids craned out the windows to see what was causing the unusual backup. Someone yelled, "Hey, Green, isn't that your dad?"

As we got closer, I could see that it wasn't Dad. It was Grandpa Green, riding his industrial-sized blue tractor down the center of Quince Orchard Road, likely headed to cut the grass over at the church. Cars pulled around him, honking impatiently. Yet, he wore a proud smile, waving in our direction. I gave a sheepish wave back. No one else's grandfather backed up traffic with a tractor.

In a small community like ours, family was everywhere. While it annoyed me, Kisha seemed to embrace it. She even started going to Grandma Green's house every morning for breakfast on her way to Quince Orchard High School. They both loved egg whites; my grandmother would fry Kisha an egg and they would sit, eat, and Grandma would share stories. Or so I'm told, because I never joined them.

Grandma was telling stories back then. I just wasn't listening. At the time, I thought I was just missing out on breakfast. But now I know I was missing out on much more.

By the time I got to high school I couldn't understand how Kisha made the time for casual chitchat with Grandma. Life had gotten really busy. I played three sports. I'd been elected to student government. I was president of our church youth group. Not to mention the homework load. There were friends to make and girls to meet. I loved my grandmother and all, but I was way too on-the-go to eat breakfast at her house *every day.*

In fact, being busy became a badge of honor. A full schedule signified importance, and I began a dirty habit of putting my family at the tail end of the priority list. They'd understand. In fact, I'm pretty sure me being busy was exactly what they wanted anyway.

I convinced myself I was doing the right thing. Paving a path forward and building my life. Slowly, the time for all of them became less and less.

My family took a trip to Disneyland; I took a pass. My father led a mission trip to Zimbabwe. I sat that one out too, complaining it was too close to the fall soccer tryouts and I needed to be around to prepare. To be fair, I was doing things I thought were vitally important. Like cementing lifelong friendships.

One time while my family was away, I had all my guy friends over. By the time I'd gotten to high school, my crew spanned the proverbial rainbow: Black, white, Asian, Jewish, Latino, and everyone's parents seemed a little more willing to send their child over to the Greens' (with the hope that some of that preacher dust might rub off on their kid). Accordingly, we often ended up at my house.

As we sat in my parents' kitchen choking down vodka and fruit punch, we laughed and clinked glasses, playing grown men. And then, like manna from heaven, the opening beats to Biggie Smalls's "Juicy" burst from the radio. I had literally been preparing for this moment. I'd recorded the song earlier and would sit in my room listening to it on repeat to memorize the lyrics verse by verse. I couldn't be outdone by my less-melanated friends.

We all started in unison, "It was all a dream. I used to read

Word Up magazine," and the collective energy in the kitchen surged. I kept my head on a swivel and my eyes alert to make sure no one slipped up. You know what I mean? When the chorus goes, "And if you don't know, now you know, N-word," I couldn't condone anyone saying the N-word that wasn't supposed to say the N-word! When that part of the song came, everyone went, "And if you don't know, now you know [silence]," with raised eyebrows and a lot of eye contact. I thought to myself, *Well done, gentlemen, well done.*

We chanted along with the song as if we somehow shared some distant connection to Biggie's story of rags to riches. Our hands, once content to hold poorly mixed drinks, now pounded the table, each beat punctuating the lyrics we'd all independently drilled into our brains. The room shook with Biggie's voice, and for a moment it felt like nothing else mattered. Until someone threw up all over the kitchen.

At the time, I thought *those* were the moments I couldn't miss. The ones that would define me. That mattered more than whatever family thing I'd skipped out on. I don't appear in many of the family photos from those years. I flip back through those albums now and sometimes wonder where I was, before remembering I chose to be anywhere else.

Journal 26–November 10, 1994

Prompt: "What's Your Highest Priority?"

In my life at this moment, my family matters the most to me . . . I know that they will always be my highest priority. I hope I'm theirs. If I had to I'd sell my soul to save them. I just wish there was some way I could tell them that.

I wrote that when I was thirteen. I didn't always act like it, but I meant it. Somewhere along the way, I just lost the thread. But the family never lost me.

In the spring of my junior year, "the Rev.," as my friends and I had begun affectionately calling my dad, approached me about a trip to Israel he was organizing for our church. He asked if I wanted to spend spring break there with him and other members of the church. I may have literally laughed out loud. Most of my friends were planning to go to Ocean City, Maryland, to talk about talking to girls. That sounded like so much more fun than wandering in the desert with my father's church group. But Dad hit me with the one-two punch.

First, he said, "Ahh, yes, Ocean City, you know we never got to go there because when I was a kid it was segregated." I'd anticipated this, but before I could make the case for why I should go precisely to make up for all that he had been denied, he knowingly interjected, "And your grandmother will be going on the Israel trip with us." That one caught me off guard.

My grandmother was eighty years old at the time, and we had lost my grandfather to cancer at eighty-one. I was worried we might lose her, too. It was a low blow from Dad, and it worked. I agreed to travel with the group to Israel. To make it more palatable, a few students my age would also make the trek.

At one point along the journey, as we visited several places where Jesus had literally walked, we stopped near the biblical city of Jericho. Dad asked me to assist him with baptisms. I tried to pretend I hadn't heard him and followed some friends into the men's locker room, where we changed into these long, nearly see-through, flowing white robes. Me, begrudgingly. I felt exposed, silly, and even more reluctant to help. It took that stern look from the Rev. that he had perfected over the years for me to join him, in the middle of the Jordan River, where Jesus had been baptized by John the Baptist.

I watched member after member of our church wade toward us, their own self-conscious hesitation disappearing into the Jordan's gentle current. My father prayed over them, and we dipped them into the Jordan. Finally, it was my grandmother's turn. She hobbled through the waist-deep cool water toward us, people she begat, her son and pastor, and his only son.

Decades earlier, Grandma had had a few toes amputated, which caused her to walk with a slight limp, but it never slowed her down. Led by spirit and with a will of steel, Grandma made her way to us. Once she was secure in our arms, the Rev. and I submerged her into the Jordan. My forearms ached, not because she was heavy, but because I was so afraid of dropping her. Water enveloped her body, and the splash from the submersion masked my tears. As we pulled her up and she carefully regained her balance, it struck me how profound it was that she was reaffirming her faith at all. I was impressed with how it was still evolving. That even at eighty she was still growing.

That day in the Jordan River, I thought I was helping her renew her faith. But looking back, she was helping me establish mine.

3

I didn't appreciate it when we were waist deep in the Jordan River, but I was already looking for my next chapter. By the time graduation was on the horizon, I was itching for change. I had started considering becoming a long-haul trucker as my ticket out of town. I saw a commercial about good pay and a pension and thought: *Maybe that's my path.* That idea was short-lived.

"So, Mom. I was thinking," I began one fall morning. "You know how I like to drive a lot?"

"Yes," she said, more like a question, hints of skepticism already brewing. I never understood how my mother knew stuff ahead of time.

"Have you seen that commercial?" I cleared my throat for confidence. "They say truck drivers make real good money and—"

"Boy, please! If you don't get your behind up to that school. And, don't forget your jacket," she said, chucking the oversized letterman jacket that I'd begged her to spend way too much money on, but was now too cool to wear, in my face.

None of my grandparents went to college. Hell, Grandpa Green never saw fifth grade, having been sent to work as a field hand by his stepmother after his father tragically died in a construction accident. But they all saw higher education as a path to better lives for their children. As fate would have it, my parents had met while walking across the quad at Mount Union College, a small Methodist school in northern Ohio. After graduation, they got married and moved to Boston, where Dad pursued graduate studies in sociology and theology. Despite my brief fantasy of the open road, which my mother quickly discarded, there were great expectations that each of us Green kids would be going to college.

Everyone in my high school class was required to attend a college fair that was hosted at the local community college. Hundreds of colleges and universities had booths at the fair, and I was overwhelmed. I wandered aimlessly through the booths, picking schools like the person who makes their March Madness picks based on mascot or college colors. Then I spotted a few classmates who were the type to have done research on how to do research before going to the college fair.

I slipped in with them. When they went to a table, I went to the table with them. Washington University in St. Louis was one of the first booths we visited. I'd never heard of it, but I filled out their card, then moved with the gaggle to the next school giving away free pens. Almost every day after, WashU sent me a piece of mail. It felt like we were old friends. When it came time to apply, WashU had become a household name, at least to me.

I was pretty indifferent about schools. I applied up and down the East Coast. If a friend was going to the University of Virginia, I applied. The cute girl from church was at Penn State? Great, I applied. Howard, Georgetown, and the University of Maryland all felt too close to home, but *what the hell*, each got an application. My mother's family hoped I'd attend their beloved Ohio State in Columbus. Boom. They got an application, too!

WashU invited me to apply to the John B. Ervin Scholars Program. It was a four-year full scholarship offered to about fifteen incoming Black students dedicated to academic excellence, leadership, and community engagement. The Ervin program appealed to me. If I was going to be at college, this seemed like a way to have a smaller, more intimate experience within the larger university. I'd be seen and supported and receive much-needed financial help. As I went through the rounds of interviews, I could feel myself transition from ambivalence to a genuine interest in WashU. It could've been my competitive spirit pushing me to want to win the scholarship competition, but by the time I received word that I was selected, WashU, a small liberal arts college with about 1,200 students per class, had summited to the top of my hodgepodge potential colleges list.

However, there was one problem. For safety and security purposes, my mother's mother, our Maw Maw, had wanted her children within a day's drive as they went off to college. My mother's version of that restriction was declaring that her children were only allowed to attend school east of the Mississippi River. WashU, nestled between the sprawling greenery of Forest Park and Clayton's chic business district, was seven miles on the wrong side of Mom's demarcation line. She was killing me with this. I knew these rules were some kind of Black mother thing, but it felt silly, a fear passed down from a different time and generation. *What does any Black mother have to worry about nowadays?* I wanted to say. In high school I remember my soccer team taking a trip to Florida. I had to keep calling Mom from pay phones along the way because she was terrified the entire trip that something would happen.

My first glimpse of WashU came after a morning flight into St. Louis's Lambert International Airport. Along with other prospective students from across the country, my parents and I were invited to campus to meet James McLeod, the dean of the School of Arts and Sciences and administrator for the Ervin Scholars program.

When we walked through Brookings and into the quadrangle, it felt like a college campus right out of central casting. Tables and chairs dotted the courtyard, and I smiled and waved at familiar faces from the interview process. Then I saw Dean McLeod. Though not physically imposing, he radiated presence. He rocked this mini-Afro with medium sideburns and a full mustache. Dean McLeod spoke in almost hushed tones, imbuing each conversation around him with significance and deliberate pacing. I thought to myself, *So this is the Great Dean McLeod.*

Right off the bat, Dean McLeod let us know his vision that students in the scholarship program and across campus would be known "by name and by story." If the campus was the community, the Ervin program was the family, comprised of students from different majors and disciplines across campus. His mission, he insisted, was to build a supportive and inclusive environment that fostered a sense of belonging and acceptance for every student.

Dean McLeod was the son of a preacher himself and modeled a student experience that was influenced by the church. It was rooted in trust and connectedness. He was brilliant. And he was Black. Both mattered to my parents. For the Greens, I'm not sure one without the other would have been sufficient. They decided I would be in good hands there with the dean and told me I could go to WashU. They hadn't lifted the west of the Mississippi ban; they simply made a Dean McLeod exception.

It was no surprise I ended up going farther away than my mom's original bounds would allow. Gaithersburg had begun to feel too familiar. I wanted a place where people didn't know my family and where there weren't so many knowing eyes. College was my chance to break away.

A few weeks before high school graduation, I was walking through the halls with Ms. Bennett, my favorite teacher and unofficial mentor. She had shaped my high school experience more than anyone else. She helped me pick classes, wrote my college recommendations, and let her classroom be my quiet sanctuary to just figure it all out. That day she was particularly proud.

As we passed my Spanish teacher in the hallway, Ms. Bennett gushed, "Jason just won the prestigious Ervin full scholarship to Washington University in St. Louis," as if it were her accomplishment as much as mine. In many ways, it was.

Señora Martinez beamed. "Oh, fantastic, you'll be playing basketball!"

Silence.

Then, trying to recover: "An Earvin 'Magic' Johnson scholarship, right?"

I was used to it by then; I'd heard it enough: "You must
play basketball." "Let me guess—post man?"

I got it. I'd had my growth spurt early. But the assumption
that folks could read me because of it wore on me. I intentionally leaned into other sports. Soccer. Volleyball. Sports that
forced people to ask more questions.

Their faces would shift from surprise to disappointment.
White people would scramble for a connection, "Oh! My
nephew plays soccer too!" Black folk were more direct: "You
play that white sport?" they'd ask, dripping with judgment.

The implication was clear: I was stepping outside the lines
I was expected to color within.

Ms. Bennett rolled her eyes at Señora Martinez, offended
on my behalf. She wasn't Black but her antennae were tuned
for microaggressions, like how she would lose her mind when
kids used the phrase "white trash."

I tried to give Señora Martinez the benefit of the doubt.
Maybe all she knew were *athletic* scholarships? Maybe where
she was from, scholarships were named after someone's first
name? I bent myself into a pretzel trying to give her an out.
The truth was harder. One of my teachers who had seen me
excel in the classroom couldn't see past a tired stereotype.

I looked forward to what Dean McLeod was building at
WashU, where people might know my name and my story.

For all my eagerness to escape, I realize I chose a college
environment that was pretty similar to what I'd left behind.
WashU, like Quince Orchard High School, was a predominantly white institution with a similar diversity makeup. I had

even found my collegiate version of Fellowship Lane in the Ervin program, another tight-knit Black community where "brother," "sister," and "cousin" were terms of chosen family rather than blood relations. And, just as Fellowship Lane existed within the broader diversity of Gaithersburg, the Ervin community was a haven within WashU's wider multicultural landscape. So much for teenage rebellion. I'd pushed Mom's geographic boundaries while staying comfortably within my cultural ones.

THE TREE-LINED PATHWAYS OF WASHU reminded me of home, even if the Gothic architecture felt foreign at first. I stumbled through those early weeks, figuring out class schedules, learning to manage my time, finding my way around campus. But it didn't take me long to settle into the rhythm of college life, especially once I understood my advantage: Dean McLeod and the culture he proselytized. He was the man. When we'd pass each other on campus he would nod and say "Mr. Green," the corner of his mouth turning upward, not quite a smile but conveying a warmth that made each interaction affirming.

He had entered Morehouse at sixteen, mastered German, lived in Austria on a Woodrow Wilson Fellowship, and now served as dean of students at WashU. His very presence behind his desk in Brookings Hall, its cascading stacks of papers notwithstanding, embodied what he preached, that all should be known by the lives they live, not the labels others applied.

More than just an administrator and mentor, Dean McLeod occupied the rare space somewhere between friend, advisor, and disciplinarian. When I served as student body vice

president during the 9/11 tragedy, I'm told that some adminis-
trators suggested holding the crisis response meetings without
us students. But Dean McLeod pushed back. He believed that
students should help shape university life, and that included the
campus response to a horrific event. He expected us to rise to
the occasion. I remember sitting in that crisis meeting with the
other members of the SGA executive team, thinking, *Well,
damn, now we better have something meaningful to contribute.*

I adopted the Dean McLeod Doctrine hook, line, and
sinker. The belief that we could be seen by our choices and our
character rather than the labels of others. I soon found myself
hyperaware of every choice. I wore my Association of Black
Students hoodie to ΣAE fraternity meetings, brought my white
roommate to Black student events, dated across racial lines,
and proudly rocked my attempt at an Afro. Each decision was
loaded with meaning, every raised eyebrow a reminder of the
boundaries I was refusing, too Black for some spaces, not Black
enough for others. But Dean McLeod had shown me what it
looked like to move with intention through all these worlds. So,
I threw myself into it all: I co-chaired the Campus Week of
Dialogue on Race Relations and helped rewrite the school constitution while taking night classes to tutor Black students on
the north side of the city. I was an Ervin Scholar and a soccer
player, member of the Association of Black Students and
brother in a historically white fraternity. I'd joined the fraternity not in spite of my values but because of them. The pledge
class looked a lot like my high school crew. That kind of mix
felt like home.

I didn't have to navigate it solo. I had an incredible circle
of sharp, fun, dedicated friends, many of whom were balanc-

ing that same tightrope between worlds. Each move felt like a statement about who we could be.

There were some consequences to all that acolyting. It cut into my class time here and there. I was busy doing important, consequential things like trying to make the campus feel like a place where everyone belonged, so I didn't necessarily see the problem. Besides, in my mind, college was obviously supposed to be harder than high school, so not performing quite as well just made sense. I had effectively been a straight-A high school student, though my older sister was the real brain. Hers were 99.5s, mine were 89.5s that got rounded up, but I refused to get a grade lower than she had. When I tensely brought home a 3.5 GPA my first semester in college, my folks seemed genuinely happy with it. And then a 3.25 the next semester was met with more praise. No one ever suggested I wasn't reaching my potential.

The summons to Dean McLeod's office came on a beautiful afternoon in the spring of my sophomore year. Originally named University Hall, Brookings Hall stood as an architectural gem inspired by the medieval courtyards of Oxford and Cambridge Colleges. When I walked through its commanding entranceway, I felt important. It was as if I'd been beckoned somewhere formidable.

When he entered his office, he flashed his characteristic half-smile and uttered his familiar "Mr. Green." I almost didn't hear him enter, as I was busy diligently rehearsing all the impressive highlights I was going to share with him. I wanted to mention the work we were trying to do within Student Union, and how recent engagement was going with alumni at the Association of Black Students, that I was interested in getting involved in the presidential debate that was going to happen on

campus between George Bush and Al Gore, and the fraternity's community engagement.

But something about his demeanor made me realize Dean
McLeod didn't have me there to talk about any of that.

He cracked open my manila folder and fed me a line I assumed he used on everyone: "Jason, we believe your future to
be among the brightest of our students . . ."

Where is he going? I wondered.

"Jason, what do you plan to do after you leave this place?"
he asked, with that paternal counselor quality I knew so well
from my father.

"Law school?" I offered, more a question than an answer. I
hadn't given it too much thought.

Growing up, we were only allowed to watch one evening
TV program, *The Cosby Show* (later we added *A Different World*).
Our exposure to the world of adult professions was effectively:
minister (Dad), teacher (Mom and Dad), doctor (Cliff Huxtable),
and lawyer (Clair Huxtable), and I guess bartender because
sometimes Mom would forget to turn the TV off and we'd get
a few minutes of *Cheers*. Anyway, we all wanted to be doctors
like Cliff Huxtable, until The Learning Channel aired a facelift
surgery. As my sisters leaned in and I wanted to throw up, ten-
year-old me was convinced that medicine was not my ministry.
So though I considered myself Theo, the seed was planted that
maybe I could be Clair.

Dean McLeod volleyed back, "Okay, which law school?"

A vague answer about "top law schools" revealed how little
thought I'd actually given to my future.

His mustache twitched involuntarily. "Well, if that's where
you want to go, don't you think you should be doing better?"

I felt the wind being knocked out of me. No one else had ever said that. Not my teachers. Not my parents. Not my friends. But once Dean McLeod said it, I couldn't unhear it. *Don't you think you should be doing better.*

Looking back, I realize Dean McLeod gave me the same gift Miss Emma gave all of us back home growing up, the gift of high expectations wrapped in genuine care. Like his gentle but firm "Mr. Green," it was a reminder that being known by name and story also meant being held to account.

Miss Emma was a fixture from my hometown and, like damn near everybody from home, was actually my grandmother's cousin somehow. Born in 1915, and every inch of five feet tall, Emma Jackson was an imposing presence. She was a no-nonsense woman with an unrelenting personality, always in a crisp housedress, her hair perfectly positioned, and trailing the scent of her famous gingersnap cookies wherever she went. Miss Emma had a quick tongue, so much so that on many occasions I heard my mother exclaim, "that Miss Emma don't play." And she didn't. Miss Emma embodied the "it takes a village" sentiment and took it on herself to make sure the village was raised right. Though she didn't have any children of her own, all the children at church belonged to her.

Each Sunday after service, our church hosted a Fellowship Hour where cookies and refreshments were served, and folks could gather, share stories, and reflect on the week. We children, after being dismissed from our respective Sunday School classrooms, would beeline for the sweet aroma of cookies. The dessert table would be a smorgasbord of shapes, colors, and flavors. I would skip past the gooey chocolate chip cookies to savor the peanut butter ones with the crisscross pattern. But one time when I was reaching for the cookie prize, Miss Emma slapped my hand. It stung and I paused, a rush of humiliation and resentment washing over me. At some point in our youth, every single one of our hands got smacked by Miss Emma. She uttered on repeat, "You know better than that! No cookies until the adults have theirs." Our parents, and I mean all the parents, respected, accepted, and appreciated Miss Emma's swift justice. And heaven help you if Miss Emma caught you goofing off during an actual service!

Like getting my hand smacked by Miss Emma, I didn't like my ego getting bruised by Dean McLeod. First came anger, then shame; understanding would come later. They both understood that real care sometimes meant reprimand. Dean McLeod could have been satisfied with my grades, he could have been impressed by how I busied myself on campus. But he cared enough to look past what I was doing to see what I was capable of. In challenging me to do better, he was practicing what he preached, knowing me not just by my name but by my story, including the chapters that weren't written yet.

4

THE ATMOSPHERE WASN'T YET ELECTRIC IN THE FLEET
Center in Boston before Barack Obama delivered the
keynote address at the 2004 Democratic National
Convention. Having graduated from WashU the previous year,
I'd plunged into the political arena as a community organizer
and was caught up in the relative fervor of the Kerry-Edwards
presidential campaign. There was an anxious murmur among
the thousands in the arena about the unknown keynote speaker.
Obviously, he was a Black man. Younger than most politicians.
But we didn't know his name. We didn't know his story. A few
minutes before he was to take the stage, convention organizers
frantically distributed glossy placards with ILLINOIS FOR OBAMA
printed on them. Delegates still grasped at the Kerry and Edwards signs; people didn't really know what to do with the
Obama ones. A loud roar bubbling up from the Illinois delega-
tion announced Senator Dick Durbin's emergence at the po-

dium. He began to emphatically introduce the newbie keynote, Barack Obama, the mostly unknown Illinois state senator who was now a candidate for U.S. Senate.

As the young senator began to weave together a narrative that felt more sermon than political speech, memories of my childhood flooded in, the comforting embrace of the pew, the resonance of my father's voice from the pulpit, a belief in what could be. Obama's striking call to embrace our better angels, to rise above the fray and strive for something greater, was food for the soul. His urgent, poetic message resounded through the Fleet Center, instantaneously acknowledging a hunger in each of us—for change, for unity, for a better tomorrow:

> Yet even as we speak, there are those who are preparing to divide us, the spin masters and negative ad peddlers who embrace the politics of anything goes. Well, I say to them tonight, there's not a liberal America and a conservative America—there's the United States of America. There's not a black America and white America and Latino America and Asian America; there's the United States of America. The pundits like to slice-and-dice our country into Red States and Blue States; Red States for Republicans, Blue States for Democrats. But I've got news for them, too. We worship an awesome God in the Blue States, and we don't like federal agents poking around our libraries in the Red States. We coach Little League in the Blue States and have gay friends in the Red States. There are patriots who opposed the war in Iraq and patriots who

supported it. We are one people, all of us pledging allegiance to the stars and stripes, all of us defending the United States of America.

I was captivated by that line: *there's not a black America and white America and Latino America and Asian America; there's the United States of America.* It tried to instantly lift the nation above the stupid labels that divide us and limit who we are and what we believe. It felt like a line that Dean McLeod or my father would have written. The force of his delivery made it feel like an invitation. There was something new and undeniably electric in the air, and it came from someone who looked like he could've been my big brother. I high-fived random strangers, wiped away tears, and made a lofty promise, less to Mr. Obama, more to myself: *I will help him run for president someday.*

I CAN'T SAY I EXPECTED someday to be just three years later.

On a chilly February 10, 2007, in Springfield, Illinois, when Barack Obama announced his candidacy for the Democratic Presidential nomination, I was just kicking off the second semester of my second year at Yale Law School in New Haven, Connecticut. I immediately began submitting my résumé to every online campaign portal that I could find. I hoped to get a job with the campaign by that summer, and maybe even defer my third year of law school while I hustled for votes.

It wasn't that I hated law school or anything. Far from it, in fact. I met and befriended some amazing people during my years in New Haven. Whether anxiously crammed into Sterling Memorial Library before finals, scouring the Bluebook on journal nights, listening to Dean Koh tell us we were off the treadmill, or stunned when Prof. Guido Calabresi tripped and somehow turned his headfirst fall into a podium into a torts lesson, they made the hard parts lighter, and I simply would not have made it through without them. And I didn't even realize yet how much I'd come to lean on them. Still, I was there fulfilling a commitment to Dean McLeod as much as anything else. I wrestled with feeling detached from my dream, however generic, of making the world a better place.

In my first days at Yale, I often felt that law school was an academic maze for which someone was cruelly hiding the map.

As a means of lecturing, many law professors used the Socratic method, a style of teaching where a professor would cold-call on students to analyze cases through a barrage of questions. I wasn't trying to be on call. Ever. In one lecture, I was particularly concerned about being called on. I had done the reading for the day's case and didn't think the conclusion followed the facts. I read it over and over, searching for the missing piece that never materialized. My imposter syndrome started to kick in, turning a case question into a deeper one about whether I belonged.

I slipped into the large classroom, adorned with imposing pictures of legal luminaries hanging on the walls, and tried to avoid eye contact with my professor. As class got started, another student raised their hand, volunteering to brief the case. I didn't know why anyone would ever do that. In briefing the material, the student confidently said, "I think the judge got this one wrong."

I perked up. *What? That's an option?*

I buried my face in my hands. That rocked me. It hadn't

once occurred to me that it was possible for the judge to get it wrong. I had put so much faith into "the system," assuming A + B always, always, always equaled C. The realization that outcomes might have little to do with the underlying facts left me grappling with a sense of WTF-ness. I felt like all this time I'd been learning how to make a good argument, but I wasn't learning how to identify, let alone change, the inequity baked into the system.

Instead of trying to master the game, I began questioning its rules. I started seeking answers beyond the classroom. I spent more and more time in the clinical offerings, which motivated me to explore avenues for effecting change, whether through community engagement, advocacy, or innovative legal approaches (which I came to realize is exactly why the clinics are there). I was inspired by classmates who were shaking the system. Some were advocating to get Yale to divest from Darfur, Sudan; others were working to change an inequitable state education system.

Searching for my own path, I found a law school clinic aimed at capitalizing New Haven Bank,* which underscored a commitment to access and outcomes for the mostly low-income communities in and around New Haven. Through the intimate act of door-to-door and organizational member surveying, we began to understand the delicate financial situation residents were facing. Some people were keeping their life savings stuffed in their mattresses, vulnerable to theft, fire, or, in some cases,

---

* When I worked on the project it was called Start Community Development Bank, but the name was subsequently changed to New Haven Bank.

tensions within the household. Domestic violence wasn't always named outright, but it was part of the quiet math that people did when deciding where and how to keep what they had. Ultimately, the clinic laid the groundwork for a community bank to be established in New Haven. It helped me start to connect all the dots and see that there could be a community-centric approach to helping deliver meaningful change in people's lives.

The summer before Obama announced his presidential campaign, I snatched an opportunity to travel to South Africa. When I was growing up, my dad had a library that I would stumble over and sometimes try to understand. Three of the authors best represented in his collection of books were Dr. King, Nelson Mandela, and Bishop Desmond Tutu. I traveled back across the Atlantic largely because Dad hadn't gotten the chance.

In Johannesburg, I could feel an energy pulsing throughout the nation as it struggled with the complexities of forging a true democracy in the aftermath of apartheid. The weight of history was so close, poignant scars were literally on people's faces as a reminder of the bloody path to that point. Despite the extreme injustices of the past, and the personal toll it had taken on so many, people were willing to give democracy a chance. It was humbling.

I worked for the Khulumani Support Group, a grassroots network helping survivors of apartheid be seen, heard, and compensated. Many had testified before the Truth and Reconciliation Commission, but years later they were still waiting for justice. Our aim was to help make justice economically viable. Some multinational corporations were reluctant to engage with South Africa due to the demands of its new South African

Constitution. Khulumani partnered with a Dutch NGO to develop tools to map human rights laws and show how inclusive growth could benefit all. My role was to utilize the tools to help businesses understand and minimize their human rights risk. The experience showed me democracy wasn't an abstract ideal but a lived reality. It was messy. Alive and only as strong as the systems built to sustain it. South Africa felt rich with the resilience of a people determined to shape their own narrative in the aftermath of profound injustice. But it was also clear that it needed to deliver.

THESE EXPERIENCES MADE SENATOR OBAMA's invitation to get involved feel like a mandate. I enthusiastically applied to join the campaign. At first, when I didn't hear back, I just sent another batch of résumés, clicking every possible VOLUNTEER AND JOIN HERE button on the Obama for America website. By summer, when I still hadn't heard anything back, I decided to accept my New York summer associateship. I found myself navigating a legal practice dichotomy. I split my time between the opulence of Wachtell, Lipton, Rosen & Katz, a prestigious law firm with high-profile clients and eye-popping billing rates. My second gig was at the Legal Aid Society, where justice seemed to move a little more slowly and resources were scarcer, but the stakes were exceedingly real. The lawyers worked out of cluttered offices and were fueled by grit and purpose. This duality exposed me to contrasting pathways within the legal field, yet neither felt like the perfect fit. The firm offered power without proximity to the people I cared most about. Legal Aid offered purpose but not always the tool or scale to move systems. I started thinking that maybe my job wasn't to choose a side but to try to bridge the gap and align access and impact. Perhaps my calling was somewhere in the middle.

I had gone into that New York summer with misplaced confidence (let's call it "the audacity of hope") and had hypothesized to too many law school friends that I would be joining the Obama campaign in the fall and thus would be postponing my 3L year. But the truth is, I never heard back from any of those résumé submissions. I showed back up in New Haven to enroll in the fall semester hoping folks would forget my prediction.

"Hey, I thought you said you were joining the campaign," person after person remarked. No one had forgotten.

Then, one day, seemingly out of the blue and long after I'd given up hope that my résumé would be selected, I received a call from the Obama campaign. The leadership team in Nevada offered me the role of Regional Field Director for the North Las Vegas office.

I felt an unexpected twinge of disappointment. I'd held a similar role in Maryland, three years earlier, during the Kerry campaign, and I'd hoped to reach the next campaign rung this time around. And *Nevada?* I hadn't known Nevada to be a presidential juggernaut, but apparently it had just been added as an early state in the Democratic presidential cycle. The primary state schedule included the Iowa caucuses, the New Hampshire primary, the Nevada caucuses, and the South Carolina primary. At the time, political pundits were sure those four states would decide the Democratic nominee. I was assured Nevada would get serious resources and attention, more than Maryland had received during Kerry.

Still, I hesitated. It was already late in the semester. The deadline to withdraw and get my tuition back had already passed. I couldn't just up and go to Nevada.

I'd spent months, unsuccessfully, trying to join the campaign, and now, seemingly out of nowhere, I had an offer. I explained my dilemma to the campaign staffer from Nevada, trying to evoke some understanding: "See the thing is, I'm a law student in New Haven, Connecticut. Your offer, which is deeply appreciated, of course, is for a role in Las Vegas, Nevada, some 2,600 miles away. Is there any chance you could maybe connect me with the team in New Hampshire? I mean, Nashua, New Hampshire, is just two hours up I-84."

I figured that staying in school and helping out in New Hampshire was a lot more feasible than dropping everything mid-semester to move cross country.

The smart-ass on the other side of the phone said, "You're in law school, right?"

"Yeah?"

"Then you understand the concept of federalism. If you're interested in Nevada, we are your people. If you're interested in New Hampshire, we can't help you."

I pulled back, looking at my phone as if I could see the staffer on the other side. *A federalism joke?*

I requested the evening to think over the job offer. I had been so inspired and so determined to be a part of Barack Obama's hope-filled mission. But I knew the campaign was a foolish undertaking. Everyone knew Senator Obama was going to lose. In the fall of 2007, he trailed Senator Hillary Clinton, the front-runner and presumptive nominee, by at least forty points. *Now they want me in Nevada?* I was preparing to say, "Thank you but no thank you."

That evening, I rewatched Barack Obama's 2004 convention speech. And again, his rhetoric lifted and motivated me. The potential of his presidency felt like a genuine opportunity to forge a coalition of Americans that transcended division. I thought he framed the choice well: "Do we participate in a politics of cynicism or a politics of hope?"

It made me feel connected to my dad and how I would creep down into the basement on Saturday nights and watch him practice his sermon delivery, basking in the green light of his Apple IIe. Dad preached, "Faith without works is dead." Joining the campaign felt like putting that faith into motion.

Obama's melodic tenor looped in my head. I believed that this was the movement of my generation. Even if it ended in defeat, I refused to miss it. The next day, I called the Nevada campaign and told them to expect me to report for work in a few days.

I've always believed it's better to beg forgiveness than to ask permission, so I didn't tell anyone at Yale that I would be leaving, except my amazing roommates who agreed to my subletting my room. I packed two suitcases and got on a flight to Las Vegas.

I was enrolled in law school in New Haven, Connecticut. I just worked in Las Vegas, Nevada.

I inherited a region and a wildly talented team of field organizers already dedicated to the area. I had been cautioned that their previous RFD had been too nice, so I came in hot. The organizers were skeptical of me and my over-calibration, but we quickly worked into a respectful routine and became Region Alpha. We were all there to do a job.

"Field" is campaign jargon for voter outreach, and our "re-

spect, empower, include" mantra meant organizing community members to build their own volunteer networks, to make
phone calls, canvass, hold community events, and get out the
message about Senator Obama's vision.

I would wake up early to squeeze in readings for law
school. As long as I kept up, I convinced myself my Las Vegas
detour was okay. My friends back in New Haven had my back,
especially my roommates, and helped keep me current and
grounded when everything else felt untethered.

But campaign life was a grind. At 9 P.M., after a full day
of voter engagement, with high-pressure goals, we'd join the
statewide team call, which was the equivalent of a high-energy
pep rally where we reported numbers, got marching orders,
and planned for the next day. We rarely left before 10 P.M. And
then it was rise, rinse, repeat.

Nevada's moment came on January 19, 2008, caucus day.
It was a three-way battle royale between Barack Obama, Hillary Clinton, and John Edwards. We had spent countless hours
organizing, training, and simulating caucuses. Then, chaos.
Caucus day was an absolute shit show, which is one of my favorite political technical terms. After all the work and sacrifice,
as the day was coming to a close it became clear we would lose
Nevada's popular vote to Hillary Clinton. But later in the evening, the campaign realized we would still win the delegate
count. And in a race for delegates, it was the delegate count
that mattered. The campaign quarters erupted. I exhaled.

The political punditry had been wrong; everyone predicted
that a primary nominee would be obvious after the four early
primary contests. But with the Nevada caucus behind us and
the primaries still raging on, my colleagues were assigned to

new states. I prepared to return to New Haven. I had done what I had committed to, but I needed to return to school. One semester on the campaign trail had been exhausting. Two felt impossible.

And I was looking forward to being a student again. I could catch up on class and be with friends and not have to worry about scrutinizing the data file or updating canvass projections.

Within a few weeks, I got a call from David Cohen, the new Connecticut State Director for the campaign. David and I had become friends in Nevada, where he had also been the State Director. He and Nate Snyder, the Deputy Director, offered me the role of Connecticut Political Director. Their logic was simple: If I could manage school and campaign from across the country, surely doing both *in* Connecticut wouldn't be a problem.

Honestly, I already missed it. There's a clarity to campaign life, a shared mission, a sense of movement. You get to pick a side and go all in. It was a refreshing break from the gray areas and legal hairsplitting of law school. It didn't take much convincing. I decided to get back in the fight.

We were down something like twelve points in Connecticut to Clinton with fourteen days to go until Super Tuesday. One of my best friends from law school was Clinton's Connecticut State Director, and our friends were split on who to support, the safe front-runner or the long-shot movement candidate.

By then we had started to incorporate mega rallies into our campaign strategy, where Senator Obama and a celebrity would rile up tens of thousands of folks and then send them canvassing door-to-door.

Knocking on doors has historically been the soul of grassroots politics. Like those banking surveys we did back in New

Haven, it let us gather insights, correct misconceptions, and build trust in the community. It wasn't glamorous, but in an era when calls go to voicemail and mail goes unread, nothing beats human connection.

Also, for Senator Obama, meeting people where they were was essential. At the start, people couldn't, or wouldn't, even say his name correctly. We fought racist conspiracy theories and the persistent belief that a Black man couldn't win in America. It took trust and time. Our organizers could light the spark, but the community had to carry the flame.

On Super Tuesday, it was Connecticut's turn to run the play. Sixteen thousand supporters packed into the XL Center in Hartford, Connecticut. Because of the Secret Service, folks had to arrive hours early and stayed in place for hours more. When the bass of the music started, the place shook with energy. Everyone knew that Senator Obama was in the building.

Backstage there was a pre-rally huddle of David, Nate, Senator Obama, Senator Ted Kennedy, Caroline Kennedy, and me. Senator Kennedy pointed out that Caroline wasn't wearing any campaign swag, so Senator Kennedy reached over, plucked the Obama pin off *my* lapel and pinned it on to hers.

My eyes darted from David to Nate like, *Y'all saw that, right?* Robbed by Ted Kennedy.

Still stunned by pingate, I almost missed David say, "Jason is going to make sure they're Fired Up and Ready to Go!"

I was shocked at the words I was hearing, but I knew what they meant and he was smart to not give me time to overthink it and chicken out. Just five minutes later, with the music blaring, I jogged onto the stage. The crowd erupted. I waved to the right. Elation. I waved to the left. Flashbulbs. One woman appeared to be in tears. And then it dawned on me: *They think I'm Barack Obama.*

Back then I had more hair. Senator Obama wasn't yet President and his image wasn't plastered everywhere. From a distance, I guess I could pass for him. That's how I received the nickname Fauxbama.

After we pulled off the come-from-behind win in Connecticut, I quit the campaign again. But then I rejoined and quit four more times. They sent me to Wisconsin, Maryland, Texas, and North Carolina. Between my campaign stretches, I'd run back to New Haven and squeeze in class time. It wasn't quite as grueling as campaigning, but it was its own kind of exhausting.

To be clear, campaigning across the country did not exempt me from Yale Law's most basic expectation: attend class. In general, I had front-loaded the strictest attendance professors in my early years. By my third year, I'd picked professors who were more predictable. My friends would let me know if a professor was nearing the G's in the roll call and I'd hustle back to campus.

On one of those trips, I was in class with Professor Drew Days, former Solicitor General, only the second Black person to hold the role, behind Thurgood Marshall. He looked across the room and said, "It looks like we have a special guest in class today."

It took a few beats for me to realize he was talking about me.

"Mr. Green, please give us an update on how things are going out in real America."

I gave a quick update, eager to sit back down. After class, he walked over, smiling. "Thank you for what you're doing. It's important." Then, almost without a pause: "You're going to drop my class, right?"

He hadn't even raised his voice, but the message landed hard. I nodded. "Of course, sir. That's why I came. I wanted to make sure I could tell you in person." That was the trade-off. I didn't get to sit in Professor Days's class, but I felt like I was being called to be part of something consequential.

Professor Days had held me to a standard. Like Dean McLeod and Miss Emma, he believed care looked like accountability, and the nod of encouragement from a man who had inhabited rooms I could only imagine showed me Yale could be a place of pressure, and growth, and grace.

After every primary contest, in the evening after all the results had rolled in, I would call my mom. We had developed a routine. We'd laugh, we'd celebrate, and we'd cry. We'd celebrate for the hope Senator Obama carried. We'd cry because history was happening. We'd cry because we were part of it.

When we won the North Carolina primary on May 6, 2008, widening our lead and strengthening Senator Obama's case for the nomination after weeks of turbulence over Rev. Jeremiah Wright, I situated myself with my box of tissues and dialed my parents' house phone. But instead of celebrating, Mom calmly said, "I'll be at your law school graduation in a few weeks. Will you be there?"

Message received.

I left Charlotte the next day and drove back to New Haven. I finished my last papers and exams. Just twenty days later, I graduated. The whole family, Grandma Green included, was there. Barack Obama was the presumptive Democratic nominee. And I got my degree. And, for a moment, I felt still.

A few moments later, campaign HQ in Chicago called. They needed someone for the general election with a legal degree and hands-on experience in field and political. Turns out all that quitting and rejoining—Nevada, Connecticut, Wisconsin, Maryland, Texas, and North Carolina—had unintentionally given me just that. I'd gotten to see the campaign from multiple angles in multiple states. And because the campaign hadn't wanted me early enough that I had to actually defer school, I ended up graduating on time and had my degree in hand.

Look at God!

With my diploma barely dry and my head still spinning from graduation, I told Jon Carson, the National Field Director, that I was in. They offered me the opportunity to serve as National Voter Registration Director to design and lead one of the first voter registration programs embedded inside a presidential campaign. The job meant building new systems, incorporating technology into our strategy, collaborating with our state field teams, training organizers, tracking compliance, and serving as a central hub for voter registration laws across the map. And we were doing it in the mold of Barack Obama himself, who had led Project Vote in 1992, a voter registration drive that proved instrumental to Carol Moseley Braun's own historic Senate victory.

That summer after graduating law school I was supposed to move home to Gaithersburg, be with my family, and start studying for the bar exam, but I moved to Chicago instead.

We had a country to register.

I was trying to live out the values I was handed. I believed almost instinctively that proximity could create possibility. That shared spaces could make people more visible to each other. That we could show a new way. That was the story I had been born into, and I believed that we had a chance to make it reality.

5

I SLIPPED OUT OF THE EEOB EARLY THAT SUNDAY AFTERNOON, Mom's worry still present in my ears. The path from my desk to the exit felt different. I felt guilty for not having spent more time with Grandma Green. Even those senior citizen proms we'd attended together while I was in high school suddenly felt like ancient history, artifacts from another time before college and law school, before the campaign, and before morning briefings were more important than family visits.

Gaithersburg, Maryland, is only thirty miles from Washington, D.C., but it might as well be a world away. Whenever I would tell D.C. people that I grew up in Gaithersburg, without fail someone would crack, "Oh, you're from the boonies."

It'd been a while since I was back home. Law school, the campaign, and now the White House had kept me busy, and living in the city meant I didn't need a car, making it even harder to get home. I'd grown accustomed to navigating D.C.'s public bus system, feeling like a cultural anthropologist on the bus to the White House and back, people-watching the wide array of riders.

I merged onto the George Washington Parkway in a friend's borrowed car and watched the marble monuments recede in the rearview mirror. By the time I hit eighty miles per hour, I was on 270 heading north and my thoughts of legal briefs and policy meetings were starting to fade.

Lakeforest Mall's sprawling complex came into view, where I'd spent countless hours girl-watching and searching for the perfect pair of baggy painter jeans. I even celebrated my sixteenth birthday at the Chi-Chi's restaurant in the mall with my closest group of friends and one of their foreign exchange students. The restaurant was long gone now, its footprint still sitting empty. It felt like a relic from another era, a reminder of how much can change while we are busy being busy.

Just a block from the mall's entrance, I made a hard right turn into the security gate at Asbury Methodist Village, a long-term care facility that was part rehabilitation center, part senior living, and part nursing home. It's where my ailing grandmother was staying.

"Hello. I'm here to visit a patient: Ms. Pearl Green."

The security guard looked at me and said with a hint of knowing, "Are you Ms. Green's grandson?" I blushed. And just like that I was back. I didn't know it yet, but I was stepping into something special. Something in her recognition of me, in her naming who I belonged to, started to pull me back into a community I'd taken for granted.

Even though the security guard gave me directions, it took a few wrong turns before I found Grandma's building. I sat nervously in the car with the engine off, collecting myself. I didn't know exactly what condition she was in. After a couple of deep breaths, I made my way through the automatic doors and entered the lobby. It all felt so familiar. The little sign-in desk. The wide corridors. The long lightbulbs illuminating the pathway.

I entered Grandma's room hugging a plant I'd just purchased in the gift shop. It was my security blanket. I figured when I walked in the plant would give me something less awkward to say than *How are you feeling?*

"Hi, Grandma!" I attempted with enthusiasm.

Grandma wore her patented smile, and she was working hard to maintain it. It was unusual to see her without one of her beautiful Sunday hats, but then again, I wasn't used to seeing our matriarch in a hospital bed. Still, she had made sure she looked good. It looked like she'd recently reapplied the red lipstick that she rarely went without. And there was my stalwart mother standing right beside her, radiating comfort. My heart was full.

"Mother, look who's here to see you!" Mom said, like a good hype woman.

My grandmother narrowed her eyes into a squint in my direction, pulling her glasses up. "Do I know who that is?" she said playfully, extending her hand for me to hold. I took her hand in mine and leaned down to give her a big kiss on the cheek. "Hi, Grandma! I couldn't resist coming to see you. How are you feeling?" Ahh, hell, I'd gone and said it anyway.

"Oh, I guess I would have to say I feel alright for ninety-five. This foot has been giving me some trouble," she said, reaching down to rub her leg. "But what else is new." She chuckled.

She quickly transitioned to me. "So, how are our President

and First Lady doing? Are you making sure everything in the White House is situated? Are they eating? Getting enough rest?" Even from her hospital bed, she fretted over the president and first lady like they were neighbors who needed tending. "They just won't let him catch a break, will they?" Grandma Green's face brightened as she fired off questions at me—her long-lost grandson—and we started to chat about my thrilling life at the White House.

My grandmother had lived long enough to see a Black man elected president, and she wanted to make sure I was keeping him safe and out of trouble. As much as I tried to disabuse her of it, you couldn't tell her that the leader of the free world and her grandbaby didn't stay in constant communication, positioned side by side, working through all the country's major problems together. And Grandma had plenty of advice for Mr. Obama too.

"Hey, Grandma. Listen here," I interrupted. "As soon as I get back to work, I will make sure to tell the president that Grandma Green said . . ."

Laughter filled the room. Grandma's joyful spirit was a welcome relief from the nerves and anxiety I'd built up about not really knowing the full picture of what we were dealing with. Which, to be honest, I still didn't know. No doctors had come by, and Mom hadn't shared any more information. As the laughter began to settle, I could tell there was something my mother wanted to do.

My mom possesses the extraordinary ability to infuse fun and creativity into the mundane. When we were kids we may not have gotten a lot of gifts at Christmas, but she would concoct some sort of scavenger hunt that would lead us from one location in the house to another, and ultimately to a present. It was so exciting, I ended up not really caring what the gift was; I just wanted to follow the clues or solve the puzzle. Or, even in church, when Dad would get a little long-winded, she would flip over her church program, where she had already prepared the dot game, and we would commence inserting lines and making boxes. Even still today, she's written a modern version of the nativity play where we all have parts and act it out after Christmas dinner. She knows how to make the most of moments.

"Mother," Mom said to Grandma, "I've always wanted to know more about your childhood. What was it like for you growing up here?"

Mom stood beside Grandma's bed with the familiarity of someone who'd crossed the in-law barrier a long time ago. She was just twenty-one years old when she married Dad and they traveled to Boston in pursuit of his graduate studies. When they returned to Maryland they stayed with Grandma and Grandpa Green. My grandparents had gifted them land upon which to build a home. However, lender after lender denied my college-educated, two-salary-household parents a mortgage. Eventually, Grandma and Grandpa Green offered to put their house up as collateral to secure a mortgage. Through the years, the connection between Grandma Green and Mom only deepened, and took on new meaning particularly after my mother's own mother passed away. I could see the effect of all those shared years.

As the conversation flowed, Mom asked more questions. "Mother, did you always know what you wanted to be when you grew up?

"What was your favorite subject in school?

"What was it like being a single mother so young?" That one intrigued me. I had never fully processed that Grandma had been a single mother.

"What's your recipe for your famous sauerkraut?" That one intrigued me less. Sauerkraut, even Grandma's famous sauerkraut with a secret pinch of brown sugar, is not for me.

I just sat in the corner and observed my grandmother's exaggerated, sweet expressions as mother and daughter-in-love played their game of question and answer. Grandma didn't seem to dwell on the struggles, though I caught glimpses. There had been employers who refused to hire her, or who underpaid her, or demeaned her. Yet, she carried on.

Their rich conversation continued late into the afternoon, weaving together a tapestry of memories, experiences, and wisdom passed down through generations. While Mom seemed to already know many of Grandma's stories, she still waited for her answers as if hearing them for the first time. She coaxed Grandma to play the greatest hits of her remarkable ninety-five years, asking the questions that animated her most.

But for me their little interview session opened a window onto a life I knew little about and began painting a fuller portrait of a woman who had lived with courage, compassion, and grace through the changing tides of nearly ten decades. I was pretty proud of the history I had been a part of in delivering Barack Obama to the White House. I'd marveled at history in the making but overlooked the living history that had been seated at my own table.

"Do you remember when I used to bring you here as a little boy?" Grandma Green's question stopped me as I was beginning to collect my things to get ready to head back to D.C.

I turned around, meeting her soft hazel eyes, and felt a twinkle of connection. The lights overhead flickered, and suddenly the memories rushed in, familiar and close, like the warm embrace of an old friend: her car parked in Grandpa's concrete garage, our counting ritual, my small hand in hers navigating these same halls. *That was it. The dream hadn't been about some office at the White House at all.*

I wasn't quite five when Grandma Green would load me into the backseat of her red car, which took up most of the little concrete garage my grandfather had built to house it. She would buckle me into the middle seat with one of those lap belts—no car seat in sight. She would hop in, turn the key in the ignition, and count to one hundred. I loved every time she'd do that because then I could show off my counting prowess. Ninety-eight. Ninety-nine. One hundred! And the car would be off. I admired her for caring enough about her things to have a routine. No matter if we were running late, Grandma Green kept her routine.

Back then Montgomery County Public Schools had a concept called half-day kindergarten; parents could choose either A.M. or P.M. school for their child. I was an A.M. kid. When my brief school day ended, the other morning kindergarteners and I piled back into the bus and were dropped off at homes like FedEx packages. Because both my parents worked, I would get dropped at my grandparents' house, just in time to watch anxiously as the Plinko chip errantly bounced and Bob Barker gave away a new car to some contestant at the end of *The Price Is Right*.

Grandma Green would make me a lunch of peanut butter and jelly and Lay's potato chips, and we would soon be shuffling out the door on our way to her volunteer work. Previously, when her mother, my great-grandmother Hallman, had been ailing later in life, Grandma Green started volunteering at Asbury to see her. And even after her mother passed away, my grand-mother continued volunteering her time there. She said she did it to be of service, to feel close to her mother and to God.

Grandma would button up my jacket, buckle me into my seat, and take me right along with her. Hand in hand we would navigate the clunky glass front doors of Asbury Methodist Vil-lage. One was always locked, and it was never the same door, and without fail it would generate one of Grandma's favorite sayings that she wielded like other people wielded curse words: "Oh, for heaven's sake."

Once we were inside, Grandma would write our names on the visitor list and distribute a few Avon books to the day attendant. Grandma was the first Black Avon lady in Mont-gomery County. She always had a stack of Avon catalogues on her and doled those pocket-sized books out like candy from a Pez dispenser. Avon, not to be confused with Mary Kay, was a cosmetics and jewelry company that employed a legion of Avon ladies, their all-female door-to-door sales team. Selling Avon seemed to be how Grandma stayed connected and built community, one catalogue at a time.

While Grandma and the desk lady exchanged pleasantries and skin care suggestions, I would race down the main hallway toward the ice room. I knew my assignment.

I was barely tall enough to open the lid on the industrial-sized ice machine. More than once it had slammed down on my back, but I learned to brace it. When it went well, I would lean deep inside to find the ergonomically shaped plastic scoop and go to town filling the bucket. I liked the simplicity of the task. Fill up the scoop with ice. Then empty my scoop into the bucket. It was hard to mess up, except one time I filled up the bucket too full and dropped the whole thing on the floor.

My grandmother would always tell me the room number she'd be in so I could work on my math to find her. As I walked down the broad corridors after the euphoria of the ice machine, I would count the room numbers and inevitably hesitate once I arrived at the right room. Even at that age, I felt a little shame that my feet would slow and my stomach would tense up as I got closer to the room number destination. *Room 332, Room 333, Room 334 . . .*

More than not wanting to get my cheeks pinched, which, to be clear, I was most definitely over, I was slow to enter the rooms my grandmother visited because they were often dark and always smelled funny. The heavy combination of antiseptic, hospital food, and soiled linens hung in the air, and the rooms felt smaller than the patients deserved. I would work up the courage to push my shoulder into the door and drag my feet over the threshold because I knew my grandmother was sitting on the other side. I realized life couldn't be all ice machines and ergonomic scoops. Some people lived in these sickly places. I had a job to do, deliver ice as though my grandmother was depending on it.

I would often find her sitting on the edge of someone's bed, or in a chair pulled close, somehow knowing exactly what to do. Her well-lotioned hands would turn the pages of a daily devotional, or silently caress a hand, or pull open the blinds to let the sunshine in. Sometimes she'd deliver one of my freshly scooped ice chips to a patient's lips, making each small gesture feel like it mattered. Often late in life, when perhaps their own families' members weren't visiting, Grandma Green served the residents a gift of dignity.

As a kindergartener, I couldn't know that most people went into this part of Asbury knowing they would never come out. But Grandma understood it. She had a way of making people feel significant and cared for, like they mattered. She did the same for me.

Back then, I was her little helper, handing out ice chips and following her lead as she made people feel seen. She taught me that presence could be its own kind of service. And it only required showing up.

And now we were back.

It was like that moment walking back into my high school a decade after graduating and everything looked familiar, but I remembered the lockers being much bigger. Asbury felt the same way: recognizable but slightly off. Memories from my younger years layered themselves over the present, and I struggled to reconcile that it was now my grandmother occupying the patient's bed. Back then, during those early visits to Asbury, I'd get anxious butterflies in my stomach, uncertain about someone's needs and at a loss for how I could help. "What can *I* do?" I'd sometimes plead to Grandma Green. She always said, "We're not here to save someone. We are here to serve someone." And I'd witnessed her service in so many ways; she was a friend, a confidant, a gossip, a distraction, a comedian, and always a pillar of faith.

With a full heart, I said my goodbyes to Mom and Grandma

and strolled back down the hallway toward Asbury's exit. I couldn't help but dissect my surroundings. All of it felt like ripples from a dream. The steady hum of the overhead fan, the pattern of the wallpaper, and the stretched silhouettes cast by those overhead lights.

6

I WALKED MY USUAL PATH THROUGH THE WHITE HOUSE COM-
plex that Monday morning. East Gate entrance, shortcut
through the Palm Room, quick stride down the West Colonnade. But my mind was still sitting beside my grandmother's
bed at Asbury. The doctors said her condition was stable, but
stable felt like an unreliable word for a ninety-five-year-old
woman with poor circulation and a terminal diagnosis. I was so
lost in thoughts of her that I didn't notice President Obama
and Reggie Love, his personal aide, tossing a football in the
Rose Garden. At least until the president spotted me, stepped
back, and launched a heave in my direction. The ball hung in
the air long enough for me to snap out of it, toss my light-green
White House–issued record notebook to the side, and leap to
make a fingertip grab.

My lawyer brain instinctively kicked in with a risk assess-
ment. What if I threw the football back and hit the president in
the nose? What if he jumped for my overthrow and sprained

an ankle? Would I have to report myself to myself? Would I have to recuse myself from investigating myself? By the time I finished gaming out all possible catastrophic scenarios, I was just standing there, frozen, with the ball still lodged in my hand. I ended up just running the football back to the president and handing it to him. I felt like that kid from *The Sandlot.*

"Good morning, Mr. President," I said with a head nod.

Reggie looked on, shaking his head in disappointment. The president looked so confused.

I collected my zombie self, bent down to collect my notebook, and wandered back out of the Rose Garden still in a bit of a trance. When colleagues asked how I was doing, I shared I'd been at the bedside of my ninety-five-year-old grandmother, listening obsessively as she and my mother took a trip down memory lane that, frankly, was simultaneously beautiful and sad. There was something about being a fly on the wall when Black women from different generations got to talking. I explained how impossibly enraptured I had been by the bits of my grandmother's story. I'd learned how much fascinating history she had touched on, and how unimpressed I was with myself that I had *never even considered* that this almost century-old person had lived a whole life before she became Grandma Green.

Everyone thought it was so cool. Hearing myself gush about my grandmother, even I thought it was kinda cool. I did decide to leave out the story about freezing with the football in front of POTUS.

A thought began to take root. Time was fleeting, and special moments with our loved ones are priceless. I'd recognized that the rarity of those family moments in my own life had been much of my own doing. I was good for sacrificing for others, but never so much for my family. They were usually the ones asked to compromise, a lesson we were implicitly taught growing up as children of a public-school teacher and a preacher. But now I was thirty-one and not getting any younger.

As the days passed, the idea began to crystallize. I wasn't sure my grandmother needed me in the same way her patients had needed her, but I thought I could be there to offer my presence, comfort, and the same quiet dignity she had given to others. I knew we had limited time, and I didn't want to look back with regrets of not having spent enough time with her when I had the chance. I felt fortunate to receive a literal wake-up call and was determined to answer it.

I scheduled time on my boss's calendar. Kathy Ruemmler was the third White House Counsel I'd had the pleasure of serving, after Greg Craig, who took the gamble and had first hired me, and Bob Bauer, with whom I'd worked closely during the campaign. I was indebted to them both; each had shaped me and made me a better lawyer. Like Greg and Bob before her, Kathy gave me room and allowed me to grow. She was a lawyer's lawyer who didn't hog the spotlight, pushed for her team to be expert, and positioned us as such in front of other principals.

She could sense I was searching for something.

"So, you're leaving me" tumbled out of her mouth before my butt had even hit the chair.

Kathy, renowned in legal circles for her prosecutorial work on the Enron case, hadn't made her career beating around the bush. I wasn't quite sure if her statement was intended to be a question or a directive. "Not exactly," I responded, hoping I still had some say in the matter. I explained that my ninety-five-year-old grandmother was sick and that I'd like to figure out a way to be with her. "To sit with her and hear her stories," I said. "I have plenty of leave saved up and thought maybe I could cobble together a little time off to do this labor of love project."

I could tell this wasn't the request Kathy had been expecting. Her face made that clear. When subordinates at the White House ask for time on their boss's calendar, it's usually either to request a pay raise or to announce a departure. In some respects, my request presented even more of a workplace challenge. Everyone in the White House was overworked and would have loved to have time off, but that was not the culture, and the responsibilities of the job just didn't really allow for it.

"You know every decision is precedent around here, so let me see what I can do," Kathy said. When she called me back in to her office a few days later, she simply said, "I think we can figure this out."

I took that as a go—I had gotten the green light for some time with my grandmother.

But like the dog that chases the car, I wasn't exactly sure what to do with the time I'd caught. In my eagerness to seize the moment, I'd jumped straight to asking for leave without even checking if Grandma would be up for sharing. It was starting to occur to me how self-serving my motivations were. My grandmother had a lifetime full of stories and had made herself available for the entirety of mine to share them. But I'd always been too busy to listen. Too busy to eat breakfast with her. Too busy with the demands of high school, then college, then law school. Too busy with the campaign and then far, far too busy with the White House. And now I wanted to show up as some sort of prodigal grandson returning to say, "I'm here now. I'm ready to listen. Tell me all the things."

My car-free life in Columbia Heights meant borrowing a friend's car for each hour-long drive to Asbury. I tried to ask multiple friends so as to not wear out my welcome with anyone. I'd built my whole routine around walking to work, hopping on and off the 52 or 54 bus and the Metro system. Now I had weeks stretching ahead of me, and no real plan beyond showing up at my grandmother's bedside hoping she'd welcome my belated interest in her life.

Fortunately for me, when I showed up for our first visit, this time armed with an ice bucket bouquet, she had all the grace of, well, a grandmother. She was happy to sit with her grandson. I'd read somewhere online that to best capture an oral history I should record the interviews. So, I bought a little handheld digital recorder, like a newspaper journalist might have, which made me feel official. I placed it on her bedside table and got right to work. I didn't really know where to start, so I just picked the beginning.

"Grandma, what can you tell me about attending school as a young girl?"

I already knew some of the story. I knew Grandma had attended the Quince Orchard Colored School, a one-room schoolhouse built on a small plot of land now known as the Pleasant View Historic Site. I tried to be sensitive with my questioning, because what did it even feel like to live long enough to see a place that you just knew as "school" now have "historic" added to it?

I had heard a little about it because every year when I was a kid we attended MayFest, which at some point got moved to

June and became JuneFest, which was a community festival that took place at Pleasant View. My grandmother's sister and her husband, my aunt Esther and uncle Curt, and their catering team would man the grills, and there would be music, arts, crafts, and games, and people from the community would come visit and tour the colored schoolhouse and the church building. I preferred staying outside kicking a soccer ball between the tombstones or helping wrap the maypole to going into that creepy old schoolhouse, but I had seen it, and my mother had grabbed my shoulder and pointed, saying "That's the one-room schoolhouse Grandma Green went to" enough times that I at least knew that much.

A small country Methodist church called the Pleasant View Methodist Episcopal Church sat next to the former colored school building. The three-acre property they rested on was purchased in 1868, not long after the Civil War ended, by three Black men for $54, for the education and spiritual enlightenment of the Black community.

The schoolhouse had come first, built with support from the Freedmen's Bureau and the dogged determination of neighbors who hauled lumber and supplies all the way from the Potomac River. In his first report, written in 1869, teacher Philip Lee recorded forty students—seventeen attending on an average day, fifteen who always arrived on time, five who had been previously free. And when asked to whom the schoolhouse belonged, he answered in flourishing cursive: The People.

The building transformed to the purpose of the day, hosting school, social activities, and church functions. The newly freed, self-determined community of my ancestors then built the small county church in 1888. That plot of land served as the epicenter of the Black community post emancipation. My father's great-grandparents, his grandparents, and a generation later, his parents were all educated at Quince Orchard Colored School. In their adult lives, they each, along with their spouses, found sanctuary in worship at the Pleasant View church.

As I sat with my grandmother, I was excited to hear more than just historical data points from her. I knew a bit about the land and the school and the church, but I wanted to understand more about the experiences.

"Grandma, what was growing up and going to Pleasant View like?"

Grandma Green's long pause deflated me. I watched as the tip of her finger traced the sheet on her bed as she accessed the recesses of her mind. I inched closer to her.

Damn it, I thought to myself. I had waited too long. Though it had been just a few weeks since she and my mother had volleyed questions and answers, I immediately assumed that I had let too much time pass and allowed the sharp mental acuity, the detail, precision, and color for which her stories had always been lauded, pass me by.

Then I felt her squeeze my hand.

"I think it was a Thursday," she began. "Yes, it was a Thursday in 1924.

"The shoes I wore pinched something awful. I was six or seven, starting first grade, and the walk from Riffle Ford down to Pleasant View felt like miles. We packed our lunches in old syrup tins. I held tight to that pail the whole way, afraid I might get sent home if I dropped it. When we got there, the teacher lined us up by age and had us sing 'Jesus Loves Me' before we did a lick of learning. I could tell schooling was important. It was different from home, but just like home, we still had our rules and our chores." She started chuckling.

Her laughter lingered in the air as I sat beside her, and the recorder continued to roll. Over the ensuing weeks, we began to talk about everything. Well, almost everything. As with any grandmother there were certain topics that just weren't up for discussion, though I worked up the nerve to ask about her first kiss.

"It was with your grandfather, of course," she replied with signature cool.

The thing to know is that my grandmother had been married once before she married my grandpa. She'd even had a child from that marriage, my uncle Howard. As we got deeper into our discussions, I learned that with Grandma Green sometimes it was best to just quit while I was ahead. She was only going to tell me what she was going to tell me, not necessarily everything I wanted to know. Seemed fair. I figured a person had earned that right when they'd lived more than nine decades.

There were also questions I carried into those sessions that I never asked. One of them was about my grandfather. I'd heard whispers that at some point he may have raised his voice or worse to her. After much contemplation, I chose not to ask, and she never said. I decided I didn't actually need to know.

By week three of our visits, Grandma and I had settled into a bit of a routine. I'd adopted Miss Emma's greeting "How you do?" and I'd gotten more comfortable with the small rituals, like adjusting her pillows or smoothing the pink, white, and blue afghan she had crocheted, which was draped across the foot of her bed. Some days she'd talk for hours about her childhood, sometimes retelling a story we'd already covered about her school lessons or her early married life. Other days her leg would give her fits of discomfort, and I would just sit with her trying not to cause too much fuss.

One Tuesday, I hadn't even reached for the recorder when she sighed, saying out of nowhere, "I miss my hometown."

"Grandma, what are you talking about?" I asked with more of an exasperated tone than I meant. But it had startled me that she was suddenly that confused. "We are in your hometown." I pointed out the window. "Asbury is right here in Gaithersburg."

"I wasn't born in Gaithersburg. I was born in Quince Orchard." Her face lit up as she said it.

Now, to be clear, I was very familiar with *Quince Orchard*. I'd graduated from *Quince Orchard* High School, which I walked or drove to depending on the day, right past my grandmother's house along *Quince Orchard* Road. So I felt I knew *Quince Orchard*. It was a high school and a road. A high school named after a road, to be more precise.

I confidently corrected her. "Grandma, Quince Orchard is a road and not a place." Perhaps visiting a place like Asbury automatically puts one on the lookout for signs of mental decline from your loved one, because again I believed I'd found senility's tell. I thought, *Now* this *is sad*.

She sensed the condescension and responded sharply, "Quince Orchard was a *place* before it was a road. Alright?" Expecting that to put the matter to bed.

Agree to disagree, Grandma, I thought. I wasn't going to argue with the woman. She didn't know what she was talking about, but I could tell I was frustrating her, and maybe she was frustrating me a little, too. We decided to wrap our session early without even turning on the recorder. I had been interviewing my grandmother for some time now, doing my best Alex Haley impression as dutiful family historian, but to what end? I was on a path, but, I wondered, to where?

I gathered my things and headed out.

Before I knew it, I was sitting in the car parked in front of my apartment in D.C., not even fully aware of how I had maneuvered home. I couldn't shake the disagreement. I'd never argued with my grandmother before. We hadn't really even had a tense moment, well, not since the great roller hockey incident of '94. But today she was clearly offended. The conversation continued to play on repeat in my mind.

Quince Orchard was a place?

Under the car's dome light, I pulled out my laptop and typed "Quince Orchard history" in the Google search bar. After weeding through countless articles about fruit and football (the QO football team had apparently gotten quite good since I graduated), I was exhausted from scrolling. But then something told me to try "Historic Quince Orchard." Somehow, I landed on the *Washington Post* archives website, and an article from 1908, the year before my grandfather was born, caught my eye.

The article, "Attractive One-Day Trips Out of Washington," was a two-page feature spread encouraging "automobilists" in Washington, D.C., to get out of the city for a country drive. The author listed several small towns in geographic order heading northwest from the D.C. border and implored the reader to go explore towns that are full of interest.

My eyes scoured the towns. *Rockville. Hunting Hill.* Then there it was, written in black-and-white newspaper text: "Quince Or-

chard is noted for its churches; Dawsonville and Darnstown [*sic*]
for nothing in particular."

Oh my God!

Seeing Quince Orchard there in print felt like a big deal. It
was validating. We were more than just a road. And I was so
happy that Grandma wasn't going senile. I just knew I needed
to get back to her. The next day, in between appointments, I
shot back to Asbury despite not being scheduled to return until
the following week. I couldn't make it down the hall fast
enough. When I burst back into Grandma's room, a nurse was
there drawing blood. She asked me to step out for a minute. As
soon as she left, I popped back in.

"Hi! How you do?" Before she could respond, I blurted
out, "Quince Orchard was once a place!" With arms extended
like I had just completed my math homework, I presented
Grandma with the evidence I had found, as if she might need
convincing. True to form, she was gracious.

"*Um-hmm*," she said, rolling her eyes a little, but then she
shot me a sly, loving grin and started to laugh.

Her laughter put me at peace. My time with my grandmother had already been incredibly meaningful and rewarding,
and I got the sense we were just getting started. "I just wanted
you to know you were right," I said, hearing how bad I still
sounded. "I mean, you knew that! But when I come back next
week, Grandma, I really want you to tell me about it. Okay?"
This time spoken with the humility I should've had from jump.

"Okay, you come on back now, you hear? And please give
the president my best. I'm rooting for him."

I walked out relieved. Grandma wasn't senile, and I wanted
to know more. I immediately jumped back into the archives and

eventually found the original land patent from the 1700s, when Henry Claggett received eight hundred acres under the original name Quench Orchard. I sat in awe, and then I started to wonder. If Quince Orchard had once been significant enough to make *The Washington Post*, notable enough to be known for its churches, real enough for my grandmother and even my father's generation to call it home, how had it disappeared so completely that I didn't know about it?

7

S INCE BEFORE I COULD SPEAK, I'VE HAD A SPECIAL RELA-
tionship with my grandmother. I love this one picture of
us from a family reunion or a Mayfest where Grandma
Green is sitting on the bench of a picnic table. My grandfather
had propped me up on her shoulders, my chubby legs straddling her neck. I'm peering directly into the camera and look
right at home nestled there, while Grandma grins. Clearly our
story began very early. But as I spent more time with her, I realized I never really thought about her life before she was my
grandmother.

The poet, lyricist, and actor Common once rapped in
"The Light," "There's so much in a name and so much more
in you." His point was that even our most loving nicknames
sometimes unintentionally diminish the fullness of a person,
confining them to a single dimension of their identity. Grandma
had always just been "Grandma" to me, and uncovering her
layers was like being introduced to a whole new person.

Grandma told me she hadn't ever expected to return to her childhood home, the Quince Orchard that I didn't yet know.

Ida Pearl was the eldest of eight, five boys and three girls. In 1939, at twenty years old, she got married and relocated with her husband Howard to an apartment in Washington, D.C., roughly thirty miles from the family homestead on Riffle Ford Road in Quince Orchard, Maryland. The young couple was renting a room from his aunt and starting to think about a child of their own. But one day Ida Pearl received notice from her mother to return to the homestead and wait on her. She worried that her mother was sick and needed her eldest child's care. When she arrived home, she realized that her mother wasn't sick. Her mother wanted her help because she had just delivered a new baby.

Grandma had stories. It was time to listen.

Mother hadn't told anyone that she was pregnant. She never told anyone when she was pregnant. I never asked her why. You see, she was a bit of a larger woman, and was always dressed in a big, drooping apron anyway so it was hard to tell and if you need to know, you would know, I guess.

When I got her postcard asking me to come home and wait on her, I believed her to be sick and in need of my care. I was just twenty-one and living with my husband Howard in an apartment at 22nd and P Street NW in Washington, that we were renting from his aunt Charlotte. I had graduated from high school in June of the previous year, and Howard and I were married in December.

When I got back home, well, my mouth just sort of fell open. Mother wasn't sick at all. She wanted my help because she had just delivered a new baby. Another sister, Esther Mae Hallman, was born right there at the homeplace, 15020 Riffle Ford Road, just like each of the children had been. Being the oldest of the bunch, I'd seen this before. After me came all the boys—first Samuel, who sadly died of meningitis just before he turned ten. I thought Mama was going to die of heartbreak.

Then came Thompkins, Upton, Melvin, and Eugene, who we all called Gene. Finally, they got another girl, Evelyn Roberta, who we call Bertie. And last but not least there was now baby Esther. Twenty-one years between me and Esther meant sometimes folks mistook her to be more my daughter rather than my sister. But soon enough I would have my own little one.

Being back at the homeplace brought back all kinds of memories of growing up on that farm. Though we weren't too far from the hustle and bustle of D.C., Quince Orchard was still country through and through. It even felt different from Rockville or even Gaithersburg.

Papa, that was my father Samuel Hallman, he owned the farm and farmhouse where I was born and raised. Now, it might sound unusual to you, but to us it wasn't uncommon for Black folks to own land back then—at least not around us. Lots of members of the family had their own place. My grandparents owned the farm right next to ours, and Papa had bought our farm from Uncle John the year I was born. That's Mama's Uncle John, not her brother John. Hard to keep it all straight.

Our house wasn't fancy but it was enough. It was four rooms—not four bedrooms, mind you, four rooms total that we all shared. By the time you came along, Jason, sometime later, you may remember your uncle Gene lived at the homeplace. Of course, he was actually your great-uncle Gene but in our family we have no place for "greats." Gene tried his best to keep the place together, but eventually it just had to be sold. She trailed off a bit.

Anyway, where was I? Oh yes, the homeplace. The house put a roof over our heads that we could be thankful for. Each of the boys grew up and left to go serve in the war. Mother couldn't bear to watch her boys go off to war, so I would go with Papa to take each one to Rockville to catch the streetcar when it was their turn to go. And by the grace of God, each returned home back from the service to the homeplace.

When Thompkins returned after World War II, he had to sleep on the couch downstairs and had to clean and put up his things every morning before the farm chores began. I would chuckle when he used to say he got more sleep stationed in Papua New Guinea, Manila, Tokyo, and places like that during the war than he did at home with all our younger brothers running around. It was his responsibility to keep the fire going in the stove all night.

You know, I don't think folks nowadays understand, but those were good times even though we had so little. Mama and Papa would make sure we had two pairs of shoes. I had my black pair to get me through all of winter and my white pair for spring and summer. It was all I needed, and we learned to make do with what we had.

When I was coming up, the downstairs of the homeplace was just two rooms—the front sitting room and the kitchen. Now, there was no indoor plumbing, so that meant bath time was in the kitchen in a big round tin basin next to the stove where we'd boil the water. And without an indoor toilet, well, let me tell you something about that! At night, if someone didn't want to brave the dark and the cold of that wooden outhouse, and Lord knows there were snakes out there sometimes, we had a bucket positioned inside. And in the morning, it was part of the chores to empty that bucket in the outhouse. That was just part of life back then.

Being the oldest, I shouldered most of the responsibility for working the farm in the early years. Papa had hogs that needed feeding, chickens that needed their eggs collected, fields that needed plowing, cows that needed milking. I remember one day feeling overwhelmed with all of my chores. I went inside and asked Mother, "Does Papa even love me, all these chores he keeps giving me?"

Mother smiled and pulled me close to her body. "Papa's tough on you, yes, but that's his way of protecting you and preparing you. We won't always be here, and Papa wants you to be ready to handle all the difficulties." She didn't say what difficulties exactly, but I knew what she meant. "But he loves you, we both do. He just shows it his way." I tell you what, making me empty the evening bucket sure was a weird way of showing love. But Papa did always say, "Life is hard. You have to work hard now so when you grow up you know how to do it right." And from then on, I did my work best I could with it. Those lessons served me well.

One Saturday in October 1940, I woke up from a terrible dream and screamed! Howard and I had just moved into our house in Lincoln Park, Rockville, that August. We'd only been there a few months when I had that dream. My scream woke Howard up and he demanded I tell him the dream—he knew my dreams had a way of coming true. I didn't want to tell him, but he was gentle and persistent about it.

Finally, I told him. I'd dreamed that he was driving our car along 355 at the intersection with Douglas Ave., with me in the passenger seat, and we were going too fast and couldn't make the turn and our car flipped over. We lay there quiet for what felt like forever. Then Howard said, "Pearl, your dreams always come true," and after breakfast he said, "I'm going to go up to Mr. Jackson in Seneca and get my hair cut." Even though it was Saturday, he put on his Sunday best. While he was up that way, he spent the day visiting all his people over in Seneca. I know he had such a wonderful day of fellowship and laughter. With everyone around him, I like to think he was able to forget all about my dream and had a smile on his face all day long.

He visited with his family on Saturday. By Monday . . . She paused. *Well, you see, I was pregnant and there was a woman in Bethesda who needed some work done and I thought it might be the only way for me to get some things for the baby. I worked a little late that day. When Howard picked me up that evening from work, we were headed up 355 and got to the Halpine Store when a car came and made a left turn right in front of us. Our car flipped. We had a canvas-top car then and I was thrown through the roof and out into the street, but the steering wheel caught Howard, trapping him.*

I could hear him calling: "Pearl! Pearl!" I checked myself and could move my arms and legs and breathe without pain. I managed to get myself to my feet and tried running back toward the car. Police lights and the firefighter's horn almost drowned out Howard's voice. But we were still talking to each other. He told me to go with the police. "I'll be alright," he said. I was stubborn and wouldn't leave until I saw him, but he was just as stubborn and kept saying, "You just make sure that baby is okay!"

This was back before they would send ambulances. So, they loaded Howard onto the back of the fire truck and carried him off toward Sandy Spring. The only place I was hurt was a mouth full of glass and a few bruises. I finally let them take me away.

They didn't take me to the hospital. They took me to Dr. Black's office right there in Rockville. He laid me on the floor, punched around on me and said the baby was still alive. Then they took me back to the courthouse where I had to sit by myself until the policeman finished his run. He asked me if I wanted him to take me to my house, but I said no, there wasn't anyone at our house in Lincoln Park. So, he drove me back up to the homeplace in Quince Orchard instead.

Situated in the police car, we carried on in silent darkness. No one had given me any update on Howard. When we got to Quince Orchard, I guided the officer to Riffle Ford Road and to make the left turn into the homeplace.

The policeman went up and knocked on the door. He asked Papa if he knew a Pearl Bell. When Papa said, "Yes," I heard him say, "Your daughter's in the car." Papa had to come out and carry me inside. The Talley boy had seen the accident on his way home and already told my parents what happened. Papa got in his car and headed down to Rockville to find out more. After they got me situated in the chair, I fell asleep and had a dream that Howard was dead. I woke up screaming and Mother had to calm me down, saying I was just upset about the accident. But when Papa walked through the bedroom door, the expression on his face told me Howard was gone. I let out a loud scream and passed out.

The next day, Papa took me to see a West Indian doctor who lived in Rockville. His way of checking on the baby was to jab my belly with his fist, almost like punches, to see if the baby would react. That was medicine back then. After examining me he said, "As far as I can see, you and the baby are fine. But, Pearl, you have to make a choice. You can forget about your late husband, forget about the accident, and bring a healthy baby into the world, or you can cry and mourn and grieve and keep that memory in front of you and bring a deformed baby into the world. That's your choice."

Some choice.

The family was tremendous and stayed with me constantly. But I knew I needed to see Howard one last time. I went to the morgue the next day. It was the first time I'd been alone since the police brought me home from the accident. I put my hand on his body until it got painfully cold. I took his hand—the hand of the man I loved, whose baby I was carrying. Everything had happened so fast, from that premonition to our joyous day

with family to the accident. It was all spinning in my head. I gave myself
that moment and then I made the choice and just moved it out of my mind.

There was to be no crying, no talking about it, nothing. My husband
was in the past until my baby was born. I wasn't even allowed to go to the
funeral. The service was at our beloved Pleasant View and then I just sat
in my bedroom and watched out the window as the funeral procession of
white horses pulled the casket up Darnestown Road toward Sugarland,
where he was buried.

The people were good to me, though. They'd take me to church
events—that was about the only place we had things back then. Your
grandfather Gerard and his first wife, Emma, were actually friends of big
Howard and mine, while he was still living. After he died, they would come
carry me and little Howard to church and things, until she got sick and
passed away. It made me sad, she'd become such a good friend. Emma and
Willie Jackson would take us too. Oh, and Anna Mae Smith was so kind.
She used to come up to Mother's and pick the baby and me up and take us
to her house for dinner. Everybody worked to keep me busy, and that's how I
got through it.

8

A S I SAT IN HER ROOM, GRANDMA'S STORIES TRANSFORMED the sterile, off-white walls into portals to Quince Orchard's past. With each visit she'd bring alive the backbone of belonging that had sustained generations. "I just love Pleasant View. Such precious memories there," she'd say, her eyes brightening.

When her family wasn't at their homeplace on Riffle Ford Road, odds were that they were at Pleasant View. As a young girl, she'd sit in the pews watching the congregation sway and rock from side to side during worship. "Once I asked Mother, 'Why do you sing so loud in church?' She chuckled and replied, 'We sing to lift our spirits and connect with something greater than ourselves.'"

Soon enough, Grandma was providing that musical accompaniment herself. She took a correspondence course from the U.S. School of Music in New York. She would play the piano and the organ for the congregation until arthritis forced her to pass the keys to her youngest sister, Esther. "I should have kept trying, though," Grandma reflected, looking down at her hands. "I think about it when I see the fellow that used to play at Germantown church; he passed just about a month ago, I believe. When he started playing, he only hit the right note every now and then. But you know what, by the end, he only had one hand but could sit at that piano and play "His Eye Is on the Sparrow" beautifully. That taught me what you have to do is keep trying and you can do it."

After the piano, Grandma threw herself into teaching Sunday School, becoming superintendent. "I didn't know nothing about being Sunday School superintendent, but someone, now I can't remember who, told me to 'just lead with love, and the rest will follow.' I tried to do that, and I've been trying to do that ever since."

Grandma taught Sunday School at Pleasant View for more than thirty years. "My mother taught Sunday School before me. I just knew growing up that I was going to be a Sunday School teacher. Even when I was married and lived in Washington, I would come back up on the weekends for Sunday School.

"My favorite day was probably Children's Day. It was the second Sunday in June!" Grandma brightened at the memory. "We'd get books from Cokesbury, and I'd write down the roles. The children would perform solos, duets, and recitations at our little church. Then we'd visit other churches and share in their Children's Day. It was just a time of togetherness."

The Pleasant View site felt like an extension of home for Grandma because between the church and the school, it felt like she spent all her time there and frankly most of the folks there were family. And sometimes school actually followed Grandma home, as teachers would board with her family. She didn't seem to mind. "I loved to learn," she'd say with a smile, "and it was much better than the alternative, which was staying home to help Mama wash diapers."

The Quince Orchard Colored School, which pulled students from across Montgomery's Upcounty area, embodied both simplicity and resilience. "It wasn't big, but it was ours," Grandma would say. "We all walked down to school from the homeplace together. The older ones carrying the younger ones, like a family on a journey of learning. One teacher would manage seven grades all in that one room. She'd teach you and give you an assignment and then move to the next group. That meant you had to be quiet, but Lord knows I loved to talk. Her punishment was me writing 'I will not talk in class' one hundred times on the chalkboard. But the teacher wouldn't let me start writing until she had her lunch," Grandma recalled. That meant "no recess for me that day. And I had to write it. A lot!"

She got so tickled talking about her punishment and then leaned back with a mix of exasperation and amusement. "You know one thing that just didn't make no sense," she said, "was how our people kept that school going all on their own. Then when the county started having public schooling for Blacks, they said they wouldn't send a teacher or lessons until the school was deeded to them. So then Gary Green and them, back in the late 1800s, had to deed it to the county for five dollars so that we could receive a segregated education. Ain't that something?" she said, shaking her head.

Despite receiving second-class resources, like hand-me-down books with pages torn out, the teachers never let that be an excuse for not learning. Their investment ran deep. Perhaps because they lived among their students and were of the community, sharing Sunday dinners and everyday trials and tribulations with the families whose children they taught. They were teaching more than what was on the printed page, investing in those stories that weren't written yet.

Back at the homeplace, the family's self-sustained farm was its own kind of classroom. From cows to fruit trees, the farm produced abundance that extended beyond their own needs. "Mother always taught us to help our neighbors. If they were short on things, we'd surprise them with jars, sending over whatever we had. It was a time when you relied on your neighbor." Grandma and her siblings would send jars filled with fruits and vegetables to neighbors in need, and the only instruction was that "they had to send those jars back so that we could send more the next year." This epitomized the essence of Quince Orchard that Grandma knew—a community bound by care and shared resources.

As she talked, Grandma painted a nostalgic picture of resilience, collective work, and responsibility. It was a community that, despite the dehumanizing realities of segregation, found strength in unity. She would craft pointed portrayals in response to my probing, but the revelations came mostly in fits and starts, like tiny pieces of a mosaic slowly taking shape. Her stories rarely followed a neat timeline. They'd start in the middle of a church service, jump back to a childhood lesson, and then fast-forward to her own children's time. And when I would question Grandma past her limit, she would guide me out the door of her Asbury room with an encouraging word, like, "If that detail interests you, then Grandma thinks you should go talk to

Mr. or Mrs. so-and-so." Or it might be Ms. Howard or Ms. Blair or Mrs. Campbell or whomever her anecdote of the day would lead me to. Each story led to another keeper of memory who could fill in another piece of the Quince Orchard puzzle.

Fortunately for me, one of the first lessons in preacher kid school is learning how to sit with folks. Before long, I'd gone to see everyone Grandma suggested and then some. I had chatted with Ms. Ada Howard, Ms. Virginia Blair, Mr. and Mrs. Ridgley, Mr. Kenneth Greene, Ms. Prather, Cousin Carolyn, Mr. and Mrs. Graham, Ms. Campbell, Uncle Howard, Cousin Sherry, Cousin Charles, Cousin Pam, Cousin Leah, Cousin Edythe, Aunt Esther, Uncle Thompkins, Aunt Roberta, Cousin Mary-Ann, Ms. Bunny, and many others. Some were white. Some were Black. All were connected through this place Quince Orchard.

Following these threads led me to Ms. Ada Howard's front door. Growing up in my hometown, I'd learned two phrases that operated like a skeleton key to open most doors: "Hi, I'm Pearl Green's grandson," or "Hi, perhaps you know my father, Rev. Green." The trick was knowing which to deploy and when. When I got to Ms. Ada's door, I chose the former. Like a secret passcode, the door swung open, and I was invited in. Kenny Johnson, Ms. Howard's grandson, and his lovely wife, Linda, were her primary caretakers. They helped Ms. Ada get situated in the front room with me.

Ms. Ada was no longer the full-figured woman captured in pictures on the wall with her late husband, James Howard. Now she was smaller and frailer, dwarfed by an oversized recliner and the two homemade comforters with her grandchildren's faces printed on them that were draped over her. We sat there quietly for a moment, and I couldn't help but think how

impossible our sitting together would have been just a generation earlier: a Black man and a white woman, almost seventy
years apart in age, face-to-face in her front room. I made small
talk to make it less awkward for us both, but she didn't need it.

Ms. Ada's words were a little hard to make out, but her
intonation was more forceful than I expected to come from her
slight frame. She spoke first, licking the chalk from her mouth
and pushing herself forward in the chair. "I just love your
grandmother. Is she well?" I relaxed. It was the kind of grace I
hadn't expected. A ninety-eight-year-old white woman genuinely checking on the well-being of my ninety-five-year-old
Black grandmother. I'd learn they had been through much together.

The parallel nature of their stories fascinated me, all the way
down to their names, branches of the same old tree, growing in
different directions but rooted in the same soil: Ida Pearl and
Ada Pauline. Ada had moved to Quince Orchard from nearby
Germantown in 1931 to marry her second cousin Jim Howard
when she was just fifteen years old. I learned that my grandparents were also cousins. My grandfather's father, Vernon, was
brothers with my grandmother's grandmother, Emma, making
my grandparents first cousins once removed, or something like
that. And, in the same way that my grandmother's family had
been in Quince Orchard for generations, so had Ms. Ada's.
Before becoming a Howard, she was a Small. And the Smalls,
as Ms. Ada would proclaim to me, "helped settle Quince Orchard." Ms. Howard's ancestor Andrew Small, in 1869, bequeathed land that would later become the Andrew Small
Academy in neighboring Darnestown.

Ada Pauline and Ida Pearl even lived across the street from each other for years while Grandma lived at the homeplace. Grandma tells a story about Ms. Ada's grumpy husband, Jim, coming across the street to the house. "He'd rap on the front door and when Mother opened it, he'd walk right past her and say, 'Where's Sam?' We would point out to Mother that he hadn't even said, 'Good morning!' And Mother would say, 'Just because someone else is rude doesn't mean you get to be. You get to control you. You still say "Good Morning."'"

Grandma Green became one of the matriarchs of Pleasant View Methodist Episcopal Church and Ms. Howard was one of the matriarchs of McDonald Chapel Methodist Episcopal South, and their parallel lives intersected at Donald Snyder's store right between their churches in the center of town. A small, weathered building at Quince Orchard's crossroads, Snyder's was cluttered with penny candy, flour, sugar, crochet needles, and neighborhood news. He'd even rigged a listening device so that his shut-in sister-in-law could listen to services at McDonald Chapel. He even had an intercom set up in the back so that his bedbound sister-in-law could participate in the worship services at McDonald Chapel. It was one of the few places in segregated Quince Orchard where people of all races interacted. The store marked both a physical and social intersection where Black and white residents' lives overlapped, if only briefly. For Grandma it's where she would make sure she had enough crochet needles. For Ms. Ada, it was where as a younger woman she'd gone to trade eggs for penny candy. Even grumpy Mr. Howard would soften his demeanor there, joining other farmers on the front porch to gossip after church.

"That store was special—cluttered, but special," Ms. Ada reflected, her voice warming. "Snyder didn't care if you were Black, white, or purple. He'd lumber out to crank the machine, pump your gas, ask about your family."

Even my grandfather, when my dad was a boy, would gather the neighborhood children early on a Halloween evening and load them up into the truck bed of his light grayish-blue Ford 150 pickup. That was back before the bottom started rusting so badly, you could see the road from the inside. The first stop would be Donald Snyder's general store, where Snyder himself would methodically study the costumes and award the child with the best costume with two pieces of candy.

Snyder's store seemed more than a commerce hub; it played a vital role in preserving the community's cohesion and rural charm amid encroaching modern conveniences. A space where the parallel worlds of Black and white Quince Orchard briefly converged, offering a glimpse of what desegregation might look like even as segregation stood firm.

I understood why Grandma sent me to hear the stories from Ms. Ada and all the others. Quince Orchard didn't live in one person's memories; it lived in the spaces in between, in the complicated ways that separate worlds touched and overlapped across generations, each holding a piece of the larger story.

9

DONALD SNYDER'S STORE SHOWED ME HOW THE COMMU-
nity could be chameleonic, shifting its appearance
depending upon who was doing the storytelling.
When I talked to Black folk about turn-of-the-century Quince
Orchard, they described it as a predominantly Black alcove.
White folks remembered it as a poor white farming outpost.
Each community acknowledged the other's existence but cast
them as bit players in their own starring narrative. Yet for the
folks who lived in Quince Orchard, their institutions were
largely identical—school, work, and church—just separated.

This parallel-yet-separate existence drew me in. Soon my
investigation into Quince Orchard had me chasing each answer into three more questions. Census documents from the
early 1900s revealed a more nuanced reality than what I'd
learned about segregation in my twelfth-grade AP U.S. history
class. Unlike the rigidly separate urban neighborhoods we had
studied, Quince Orchard's population formed an unusual

checkerboard pattern. Black and white families lived side by side as both owners and renters of their property. My grandmother's father, for instance, owned his farm in 1940, surrounded by Black and white neighbors who both rented and owned on all sides.

The churches for which Quince Orchard was noted best told this story of separation and proximity.

The Pleasant View Methodist Episcopal Church congregation began worshipping in a little house even before construction began in 1868 on the one-room schoolhouse, one of the first institutions in the area established by newly freed people. My ancestors constructed log cabins along the road between Quince Orchard and Darnestown, much like other early settlers in the community. When they had saved enough money to build Pleasant View's permanent church structure in 1888, it became both a spiritual home and a symbol of Black self-determination. Though the congregation would continue to worship and lead with independence and grace, in the decades that followed, Pleasant View would fall under the Methodist Church's segregated Central Jurisdiction, a reminder that even faith was divided.

McDonald Chapel Methodist Episcopal Church South arrived in 1901. Rev. William A. McDonald, pastor of Grace Methodist Episcopal Church South in Gaithersburg, had overseen the establishment of a mission house of worship in Quince Orchard but died before its completion. When the new 250-seat church was dedicated in 1903, it was named McDonald Chapel in his memory. The "South" in Methodist Episcopal Church South stemmed from the denomination's 1844 split over slavery. Maryland's precarious position as a non-seceding slave-owning state meant it hosted both antislavery Methodist churches and pro-slavery Methodist South congregations, and those divisions would persist beyond emancipation.

Finally, the cornerstone for Hunting Hill Methodist Episcopal was set in 1902. Hunting Hill was a very small rural church with an all-white farming congregation. The church was on a charge with the Gaithersburg Methodist Episcopal circuit, but the building itself had been reconstructed from a razed church in west Rockville, the building having been brought out piece by piece.

Given the rosy anecdotes shared by surviving elders who remembered the time past, I had to resist the urge to elevate Quince Orchard into some rarefied realm of race-relation. Their actual worlds, though adjacent and similar, had remained largely segregated, each rooted in its own nucleus of faith and community. This toggle between racial segregation and integration defined Quince Orchard life, creating moments of racial progress and violent backlash.

In May of 1880, my great-great-grandfather (depending upon which branch you take) Gary Green was elected as an alternate delegate from Quince Orchard to the Republican Presidential Convention, a seemingly remarkable achievement just fifteen years after the Civil War. But in that same year, only months after Gary's election, John Diggs-Dorsey, another Black man from the same community, would be killed by racial terror.

Mr. Diggs-Dorsey, a twenty-three-year-old Black man, was accused of assaulting a white woman in Darnestown and was detained by the sheriff in Rockville. A white mob is believed to have traveled through Quince Orchard to abduct him from the

Rockville jail, march him in his leg-irons to a place one mile outside of Rockville, and lynch him before returning home up Darnestown Road through Quince Orchard. It's quite possible Mr. Diggs-Dorsey attended the Quince Orchard Colored School, or the Pleasant View Methodist Episcopal Church, or had been a contemporary of my great-great-grandfather's. The perpetrators of the heinous crime were never brought to justice. Both the local jury of inquest and the grand jury returned a verdict of death by "violence committed by parties unknown." Some newspaper accounts hailed the outcome as just and deserved.

Almost two decades later, another noteworthy racial cornerstone moment took place in Quince Orchard. In 1899, John Ricks, believed to be my relative, received a historic appointment as what appears to be one of the first colored postmasters in the North. The big news was carried in regional newspapers, including the *Denton Journal* on the Eastern Shore. "The administration at Washington is moving north with the colored postmaster, heretofore exclusively known in the South. A few days ago, John Ricks, colored, was appointed postmaster at Quince Orchard, Montgomery County, Md." Given that even Abraham Lincoln had used a postmaster position as a stepping stone to politics, this appointment suggested an unusual degree of racial conciliation in Quince Orchard.

But my high didn't last for long. The very same day that I discovered Ricks's historic appointment, another news story jerked me back to earth. In 1901, just two short years later, arson destroyed the original Quince Orchard Colored schoolhouse, apparently in backlash against political activity by the "Negro school teacher." Undeterred, the Black community demanded a new school, and insurance money was used to build one. However, the new school went to the white students, and the old white school was dragged across Darnestown Road to the Pleasant View site. Not only did the Black students receive hand-me-down books, but they also got a hand-me-down school. "Thank goodness our teachers and our families always told us we were just as good as anyone else," Grandma said. "And it actually showed me we were equal. If the white students had used that school the day before, we were just as good."

Quince Orchard wasn't exactly the racial outlier I had thought that it might be. As I combed through the archives and peppered the elders with questions, it had become undeniably clear that, like many other early American communities, and the arc of American history more broadly, Quince Orchard experienced moments of progress and corresponding backlash. Yet even amid those setbacks, progress found ways to take root.

Pleasant View, McDonald Chapel, and Hunting Hill weren't just important physical structures; they embodied the human legacy of Quince Orchard. As Pleasant View served as the heartbeat of Methodist Black life, McDonald Chapel and Hunting Hill played similar roles for the white communities. They captured the life cycle of the community—the memories, spirit, challenges, hardship, and camaraderie. For my family, especially my grandmother, Pleasant View hadn't been just a church; it *was* Quince Orchard itself.

"This is where our family has been rooted for a long time," Grandma Green said, sitting on the edge of her bed and looking straight into my eyes. It's home. That simple statement of fact encapsulated her deep sense of belonging in a community marked by advances and atrocities.

At first, I hadn't known what so compelled me to go down the Quince Orchard rabbit hole. But Grandma's mention of our family being tethered to this land—belonging to it—for so long sparked a childhood memory I'd tried to leave behind.

ONE AFTERNOON IN SIXTH OR seventh grade, I ambled my way home after school. About halfway down the street, I felt a sense of unease creep over me. Clasping my backpack straps, I turned slightly to see over my left shoulder a group of older white kids about forty yards back. No words were exchanged, but my instincts had kicked in, urging me to pick up my pace. After a few more steps, unable to resist, I looked back again. One of the boys didn't like that and started sprinting toward me.

I wish I could say I sidestepped his advance, grabbed him by the arm, and flipped him over me while all his friends stared on in wonder. I've had that fantasy once or twice over the last twenty-five years. But that's not how it went down.

Instead, I froze. I didn't start running or even keep walking. I just stood there, feet firmly planted, watching as this kid stormed down the hill in my direction. When he reached me and realized that I was about the same height as him, it seemed to enrage him more. His dark eyes flashed, and he started to spew a torrent of hate. "Get out of here!" I didn't move. Then, with rising fury: "I said get out of here, nigger!"

The slur sounded unpracticed; he almost swallowed it on delivery. Maybe it was his first time. Maybe I *was* the practice. Had I known who this dark-haired kid in an Adidas tracksuit was, if we'd had any history at all, then maybe I would have been able to muster the venom to match his. But I'd never even seen him before, and hard as I tried to look tough, I was more confused than anything. I couldn't fathom how he had such hateful feelings without knowing anything about me.

His words had been frenetic, but he eventually found his refrain: "You don't belong here!" He repeated it again, growing louder and getting into my face as if the intensity alone would make it real. "You don't belong here!"

The irony on a street that my family had literally named.

I slowly backed away from the group, heading toward my house. He kept yelling at me to go run off, but I wouldn't turn my back to break eye contact. Preserving some semblance of dignity, I refused to give him the satisfaction of running away. Whatever he was going to say or do, I wanted it to be said or done to my face.

Finally, with the confidence of his friends standing behind him, and me halfway up my driveway, he launched a final: "You don't belong here, nigger!"

When I made it home, I was visibly shaken up. My mother grabbed me and asked what happened. "What'd they do? What'd they say?" she instinctively asked. I couldn't answer her. She pulled my body close to hers into an embracing hug and then pushed me away so she could examine me fully. No cuts. No marks. At least none that were visible. "What happened?" Her voice reached a new pitch. I never answered her.

We both cried. My tears were out of anger and confusion, hers seemingly out of relief that I was unharmed. To this day, we have never spoken about it.

But that boy's voice has crept in to other rooms, making me ask: *Do I belong?*

10

I T WAS LATE SPRING 2013, AND MY LEAVE WAS UP.

I had missed it. I missed the building, the people, and the mission. But something had shifted. The White House hadn't changed. It was me.

My body was in Washington, D.C., but my head was back in Quince Orchard, trying to pull threads and piece stories together.

When I got back to work, Grandma Green's lessons kept surfacing. Her voice seemed more urgent than whatever room I was in. Definitely not ideal for a position where part of my job was being in the details and making sure the wrong things didn't end up on the front page of *The Washington Post*.

After days of hand-wringing and nights full of questions, I emailed Kathy's assistant, again, to get more time on her calendar.

The Counsel's office was on the top floor of the West Wing. Typically, I'd bound up the stairs, sometimes two at a time. But on this trip to my boss's office, I slowly counted each step. I greeted the office assistants and quietly took a seat to wait for Kathy. When the door opened, Attorney General Eric Holder emerged from the office and gave me the nod on his way out. Kathy waved me in. *Life is wild,* I thought.

"So, you're leaving me?" Kathy started in again.

This time I was pretty sure it was a question.

"Yes," I muttered. "I think it might be time for me to go." I'd rehearsed what to say, but it all disappeared. So, I just kept it real. I told her my grandmother was still at Asbury, and all about how the weeks I'd spent with her had made me question a lot and want to know more. I explained that I felt almost haunted. I wasn't going to get this time back. I couldn't just put Grandma off for later again. I'd done that already. She was a griot, genuine living history—I needed to be by her side and collect her stories, both for me and to pass on to my family. When it came down to it, the White House was a once-in-a-lifetime opportunity, but so was Grandma Green.

Kathy listened, nodding her head with understanding and genuine empathy. Then she asked, "But how will you make money?"

Now that was a damn good question and one I had, perhaps naïvely, pushed aside. I'd been focused on memory and meaning at the expense of financial security. Even with student loans and D.C. rent looming, I'd convinced myself that pursuing purpose would somehow allow the money to work itself out. Her question had landed like a firm slap in the face, though. I tried to shake it off. "I'll figure that part out," I said as confidently as I could. This was something I had to do, though I was still not exactly sure what *this* was.

"Well, you're either very smart or very dumb, but I can tell you need to go figure that out on your own."

I wandered out of her office. Did I just quit my good government job, as my mom would say? And did my boss just quote *Enemy of the State*? My head was spinning.

Weeks later, administration colleagues convened for my farewell ceremony in the Indian Treaty Room on the fourth floor of the Old Executive Office Building, which is the most beautifully ornate room, though as I understand it no Indian treaties were ever signed there. The room buzzed with lawyers, policy wonks, and political strategists—friends. I hoped these relationships would endure as I embarked on the next chapter. Leaving was bittersweet, like saying goodbye to a first love. I was full of gratitude, doubt, and fear. We reminisced about the good times and the storms we'd survived. Hearing the kind words spoken about me was humbling and an honor. As the champagne poured, someone passed me the microphone.

I smiled and fought back tears. "Being here with all of you has been the time of my life. From knocking on doors in Nevada to election night, from healthcare through the reelect, we have been on this crazy ride together and gotten to serve the American people and shock the world at the same time. I know everyone's busy, so the fact that you're here means so much. Working alongside you was the best part of my everyday . . ." I paused, uncertain how to proceed, as I'd come to the part of the program where the departing staffer usually announces their fancy new job. "I'm smiling because none of you know what I'm going to do next. I'm going to go spend some time with my grandmother."

A puzzled expression spread across nearly everyone's face,

followed by a swell of forced smiles. Maybe they were genuine. Maybe they were just surprised. Or maybe I just wasn't ready to believe that this kind of choice would be seen as strong.

I quickly raised my glass higher and cheersed, "Thank you for everything."

For the final time, I took the stairs two stories back down to my office to gather the last remnants of more than four years of my work life, finish archiving my emails, and turn in my beloved badge and BlackBerry. My tackboard had become a time capsule of inside jokes, shared victories, and personal inspiration. Doubts started to creep in. Was I making a mistake? They say you only leave the White House once, better do it right.

One of the cleaning staff knocked on my door. She was an aging Black woman, her graying hair pulled back in a neat twist and a voice that could soften the hardest day. Her name now escapes me, but I knew it then. She had been supplying me with steady smiles and hellos for years as she cleared our trash cans and burn bags. She had heard that I was leaving and said, "I think what you're doing is beautiful. When my grandmother passed, all the stories went with her. It just eats me up inside."

I hugged her and thanked her. It was exactly the validation I needed.

There was just one more thing to do. I called my mother. Mom still wasn't sold on the idea of me leaving.

"You can't leave the White House! What will they do without you?" she joked but said with all seriousness.

"Mom, trust me, the White House will be fine."

"Okay, okay. But we haven't even met President Obama yet," she said.

Aha! The real concern had come out. "Well, did you know that when a staffer departs the White House, they're able to bring their family in to meet with the president for a photo?"

"What? Oh, you're long overdue to leave the White House," Mom teased. "Isn't that place stifling your growth? It's been more than four years, ya know? Might be time for you to find something else to do!"

She didn't yet know that that "something else" would eventually have me back sleeping in my childhood bedroom, but I appreciated the sentiment.

"So, what *are* you gonna do?" Mom asked.

"I'm not sure yet, but in the meantime, I thought I could go be with Grandma."

"Aww, back at Asbury like when you were a boy." Her warm tone comforted me. "But what will you do for money?"

Again, I had no good answer, so I employed the time-tested Washington strategy—ignore and pivot. I told her I had to get back to packing things up but that I would be following up regarding the planning for our departure picture.

When the time came, I was nervous. Less to take a picture with the president, and more to see how my family would interact with him. We had a large group. Most folks are able to bring their parents and a partner. Somehow, I had my parents, my two sisters, my sister's husband, their two kids, and my grandmother in a wheelchair.

I met my family at the North Gate to help navigate security. I watched as my father proudly pushed my grandmother's wheelchair up the north driveway, past the Marine guard standing at attention, and into the West Wing lobby. She was wearing a beautiful new black skirt suit with embroidered tan trim that my mom had gotten her. And, of course, she wore a matching black church hat with a rose on her right side.

Other families were already waiting in line, but we were first on the schedule. Everyone remarked about how large our group was and made space as more family members continued to process through the door.

As we paced the waiting room, I could see my five-year-old nephew, Spencer, starting to get rambunctious. I called him over to me and said, "I need you to be on your best behavior today, bud. Okay?"

"Mommy said that we are going to meet your boss today. Is that true?"

"Yeah, bud, that's true."

"But where are we?" he squealed.

I squatted down to his level. "We are at the White House. You know I work at the White House." Spencer had been to all the White House Easter Egg Rolls.

Spencer had more questions. "Does President Obama work at the White House?" he asked as the corners of his mouth started turning up.

"Yes."

"Is President Obama your boss?"

"Yes, he is." I could see his little mind working the syllogism to ask the next, and most important, question.

"Are we going to meet President Obama?"

"Yeah, bud, we are."

He paused, taking in my answer. Without me even having to press him, he assured me, "I'll be good." And he sat right down in the chair.

And then it was time to go in.

Guiding the group into the outer oval area, I exchanged greetings with President Obama and introduced him to all the members of my family. "Mr. President, please meet my mother, Mrs. Rita Green; my father, Rev. Gerard Green; and my grandmother, Mrs. Ida Pearl Green, who is ninety-five years young." Grandma was looking up from her wheelchair and her face radiated with joy as the first Black President reached to shake her hand. Determined to stand out of respect, she tried to rise out of her wheelchair. President Obama assured her she didn't need to get up just for him. For a hilarious few seconds, they were in a push-of-war, Grandma attempting to stand while President Obama gently pushed her back into the chair, until she finally relented.

Next the president scooped up my two-year-old nephew, Byron, into his arms. Witnessing Spencer and Byron marvel at his presence made us all choke up. Their hopeful, innocent little Black boy eyes seemed to grasp the significance of the moment. As the entire family filed into the Oval Office, I gave the quick stats of my starting team, "This is my sister Kisha; she's a family physician. My other sister, Maya, is finishing up her medical residency." The president looked at my parents and said, "I don't know what y'all were serving over at the Green household, but can I get some?"

Mom and Dad blushed.

A minister for most of my life, my father had always found the right words regardless of the occasion. Whether to inspire me on my darkest day, celebrate the union between two beloveds, or send a loved one to the hereafter, words came natural to him. But this time, glowing with pride, Dad extended his hand to the president and said, simply, "Thank you."

The president accepted my father's gratitude and turned to the rest of the family for pictures. Pete Souza, the president's photographer, efficiently organized us in front of the resolute desk across from the Emancipation Proclamation hanging over the Martin Luther King bust and did his magic. Glancing over at Dad, I sensed his disappointment. This man of many words had only managed to utter two to the leader of the free world.

Following the photo session, the president positioned himself to shake hands and say thank you to each of my family members as they departed. As he said goodbye to my father, the president said, "Thank you, Reverend Green."

"Thank you, Mr. President," the Rev. managed this time as he shook President Obama's hand. But it seemed that Dad still wasn't entirely satisfied with himself. Perhaps he had crafted a blessing or a prayer to share with the president, something to shield him from both known and unknown adversaries, a message to maintain the faith. Observing my father and the president shake hands reminded me of what had drawn me to the president in the first place.

When I sat in the Boston convention hall in 2004, a younger Barack Obama roused the crowd with his message of community, hope, and prosperity, and reminded me of a younger Gerard Green, who would evoke emotion in his congregants by imploring that they were all part of a single human fabric and capable of far more together than apart. My dad's simple thank you to the president was really thanking him for taking the baton of hope to the next level, and to me it conveyed all the sentiment, faith, and vision that any prayer could have given. It was clear to me he had found exactly the right words.

"Greens, thank you for lending us Jason. He's been a valuable member of the team, and we know he is going to go on to do great things at . . . wait, Jason, remind me where you're going?" I hadn't planned for this awkward moment. We had gone to great pains to not tell my grandmother I was leaving the White House to spend time with her. She just wouldn't have allowed it. She was always under the impression that the doctors were wrong and she would leave Asbury. So when the president asked, I couldn't say, "To my grandmother's room."

Instead, I said, "Oh, I'm just going to take a little time off."

This answer disappointed both Grandma and the president. My grandmother, who at ninety-five years old still worked as an Avon lady, even from Asbury, and had rarely, if ever, taken a day off, looked at me with a scowl. President Obama said what she must have been thinking: "Some time off? Time off? I want some time off!"

I smiled sheepishly, thanked him again, and quickly shooed the family out of the Oval Office. Once we got Grandma out of earshot, I doubled back to tell the president I was actually going to spend time with her, as he had done on the campaign with his own grandmother. He exhaled a sigh of relief. We shared one last bro hug. I savored that.

After working for him for six years, between the campaign and the White House, it was time for me to figure out who I was without Barack Obama behind me, and to find my own way forward.

11

O N THURSDAY, APRIL 4, 1968, THE EVENING SKY WAS
veiled with clouds, and a slight drizzle had just started
as congregants arrived at Pleasant View. The cemetery with its scattered, protruding tombstones felt particularly
ominous as a partially obscured crescent moon cast long eerie
shadows. The gravel parking lot loudly announced each car
that approached before its inhabitants were even known. Congregants parked closer to the schoolhouse door than normal to
scurry inside with erect raincoat collars and extended umbrel-
las. The members of the church were meeting over in the
schoolhouse purchased the same month one hundred years
earlier, but this was no anniversary celebration.

Members of the Christian women's coalition arrived first,
per usual, and set the table for congregants to place their pot-
luck items like country fried chicken, potato salad, Evelyn Hallman's famous desserts. As folks shuffled in, the century-old
floorboards creaked almost as loudly as the congregants they

supported. Rain slickers and top hats were whisked off and slung on hooks hand-carved and fastened generations earlier.

For months, Thompkins and Melvin Hallman, two of Ida Pearl's five younger brothers, had tried to inform the congregants of Pleasant View Methodist Episcopal Church that their financial woes, created by their membership woes, would continue to persist. They would not be able to survive on their own much longer. Resiliently, since Pleasant View's remarkable inception in the late 1800s, the church had always been able to find a way to survive.

Pleasant View was founded in the wake of emancipation. Though its official records begin in 1868, it's widely believed that Black folk in Quince Orchard gathered for worship long before then, quietly studying scripture, building faith, and living the gospel. The schoolhouse came first. For two decades, it served double duty as a place for educating children and for saving souls on evenings and weekends, until the community saved enough money to build a proper church building roughly fifty yards southeast of the schoolhouse. Like a superhero and her sidekick, those two buildings stood watch over the Black community of Quince Orchard for generations.

The evening's dinner topic was church survival, and the mood was somber, but not because it had already been decided that survival was beyond reach. It was somber because to date the church had been able to meet any challenge presented. The church community had saved the money to build the church in the first place. Local men had hand-carved and installed the pews, though slightly askew, in the sanctuary. When a portion of the church needed to be rebuilt, the community came together to underwrite the effort. The trustees raised the funds and oversaw a more recent sanctuary expansion project. The church had made a habit of providing for itself, and if survival was a real question, then the congregants would have to look internally and face how it had come to this.

Fried-chicken dinners and pancake suppers, with fresh ingredients picked from Quince Orchard farms, were no longer effective fundraisers. With a dwindling population, it seemed like the very people delivering those fresh ingredients for the dinners were the same people making the dinners and the same people buying the dinners. Hard to turn any profit that way.

Ironically, younger generations were doing precisely what they had been told to do, to a fault. They were matriculating into higher education, joining the military, and pursuing new opportunities, which included moving off the farm and often toward Washington, D.C., and Baltimore. Thompkins and Melvin had the difficult but necessary responsibility to tell the congregation what study after study had already revealed: Pleasant View didn't have the congregational population or pipeline to be able to survive as a standalone church for much longer.

They offered options for the Pleasant View congregation to consider. It was hard to call each alternative viable, but they were the last options. One option was to merge with the Black congregation with which they had recently shared a minister. Pleasant View had been in a "charge relationship" with Emory Grove Methodist Episcopal Church, which meant the same minister would preach at each church—one after the other— and the minister's salary would be split between the two congregations. But Emory Grove was all the way on the other side of Gaithersburg, and the distance alone made it feel like a stretch. That, combined with a general sense of underwhelm—Pleasant View felt the pastor was giving Emory Grove more attention than Pleasant View—with the joint pastor, made the Emory Grove option unlikely.

Other congregants, including Gerard Green, Sr., argued for the tried-and-true strategy of continuing as a small independent church and praying things would work out. Pleasant View, as a faith-based institution, fundamentally believed in the power of prayer, and their prayers had been answered in the past. Without a prayer being answered, the congregants knew this approach, of not changing anything, would at some point, likely sooner than later, lead Pleasant View to shut its doors.

Another option was to merge with two other Methodist congregations, each located within a few miles of Pleasant View in Quince Orchard. The problem was they were white, and the two white congregations did not even seem to get along themselves. McDonald Chapel and Hunting Hill were on a charge relationship and had previously tried and failed to integrate some of their functions. One was "northern" and one was "southern." A stark reminder of the Methodist Church's decision to split over the issue of slavery.

There were no perfect options.

On one side of the room, Emma Jackson, draped in her church apron, busied herself making space on the serving table and placing items from the makeshift kitchen. On the other side, a few church elders had already found their way to a set of chairs. Dressed in overalls and crisp white shirts, the elders discussed the spring's crop and whether one of the youngsters would come plant their cornfields. When Peachy, Gerard Green's son, entered the room, he could feel the farmers look

Matilda Mason Green

Gary Green

RECORD OF SLAVES IN MONTGOMERY COUNTY, At the Time of the Adoption of the Constitution in 1864.

Maryland Record of Slaves, Samuel Higgins–Matilda Green, 1867

RECORD OF SLAVES IN MONTGOMERY COUNTY, At the Time of the Adoption of the Constitution in 1864.

Maryland Record of Slaves, John H. Higgins–Gary Green, 1867

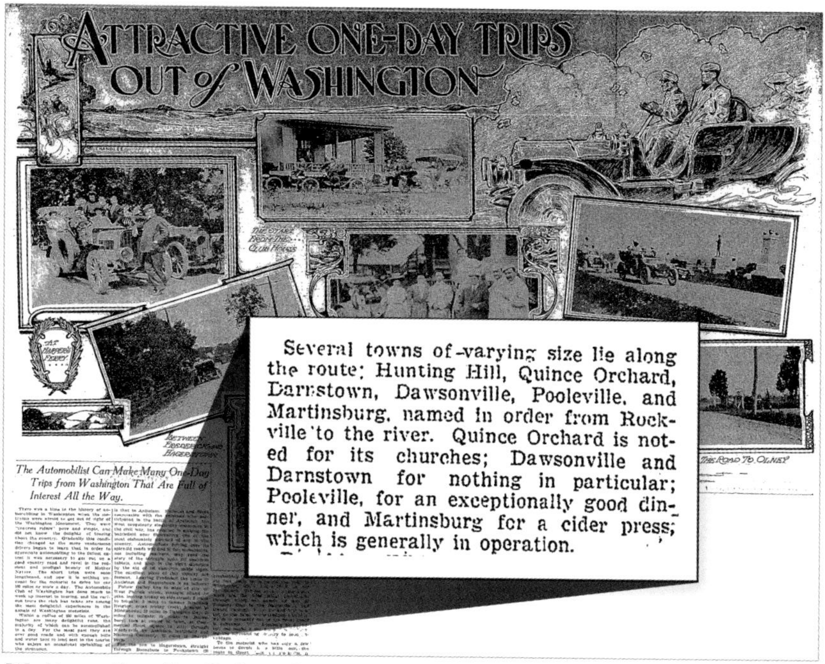

ATTRACTIVE ONE-DAY TRIPS OUT of WASHINGTON

The Automobilist Can Make Many One-Day Trips from Washington That Are Full of Interest All the Way.

Several towns of varying size lie along the route: Hunting Hill, Quince Orchard, Darnstown, Dawsonville, Pooleville, and Martinsburg, named in order from Rockville to the river. Quince Orchard is noted for its churches; Dawsonville and Darnstown for nothing in particular; Pooleville, for an exceptionally good dinner, and Martinsburg for a cider press, which is generally in operation.

Washington Post clip, Quince Orchard, 1909

STATE OF MARYLAND
CERTIFICATE OF DEATH

1033 (77)

1 PLACE OF DEATH
County Montgomery
Registration Dist. No. 215
Village or City near Darnestown (No. .... St.; .... Ward)
[If death occurred in a hospital or institution, give its NAME instead of street and number.]

2 FULL NAME Lettie Matilda Green

PERSONAL AND STATISTICAL PARTICULARS

3 SEX Female
4 COLOR OR RACE Negro
5 SINGLE, MARRIED, WIDOWED OR DIVORCED (Write the word) Widowed
6 DATE OF BIRTH 3rd (Month) unknown (Day), 1833 (Year)
7 AGE 84 yrs. 10 mos. — ds. If LESS than 1 day, ... hrs. or ... min.?
8 OCCUPATION (a) Trade, profession, or particular kind of work Housewife
(b) General nature of industry, business, or establishment in which employed (or employer) —
9 BIRTHPLACE (State or country) Montgomery Co
PARENTS
10 NAME OF FATHER Nathan Mason
11 BIRTHPLACE OF FATHER (State or country) Montgomery Co
12 MAIDEN NAME OF MOTHER Lucy (Unknown)
13 BIRTHPLACE OF MOTHER (State or country) Montg. Co
14 THE ABOVE IS TRUE TO THE BEST OF MY KNOWLEDGE
(Informant) Vernon Green
(Address) R.F.D. Germantown Md
15 Filed 1/12, 1918 U. D. ... Registrar

MEDICAL CERTIFICATE OF DEATH

16 DATE OF DEATH 1st (Month) 11 (Day), 1918 (Year)
17 I HEREBY CERTIFY, That I attended deceased from Dec 15, 1917, to Jan 8th, 1918,
that I last saw her alive on Jan 8, 1918,
and that death occurred on the date stated above, at 8 P.m.
The CAUSE OF DEATH* was as follows:
Chronic valvular heart disease (Aortic regurgitant)
(Duration) 10 yrs. — mos. — ds.
Contributory (Secondary) Senile decay.
(Duration) ... yrs. ... mos. ... ds.
(Signed) U. D. House, M.D.
1/12, 1918 (Address) Dawsonville Md
*State the Disease Causing Death, or, in deaths from Violent Causes, state (1) Means of Injury; and (2) whether Accidental, Suicidal, or Homicidal.
18 LENGTH OF RESIDENCE (For Hospitals, Institutions, Transients, or Recent Residents)
At place of death ... yrs. ... mos. ... ds. In the State ... yrs. ... mos. ... ds.
Where was disease contracted, if not at place of death?
Former or usual residence
19 PLACE OF BURIAL OR REMOVAL Quince Orchard Mont. Co.
DATE OF BURIAL 1/14, 1918
20 UNDERTAKER Rubi Pumphrey
ADDRESS Rockville Md

MARGIN RESERVED FOR BINDING
WRITE PLAINLY, WITH UNFADING INK—THIS IS A PERMANENT RECORD
N. B.—Every item of information should be carefully supplied. AGE should be stated EXACTLY. PHYSICIANS should state CAUSE OF DEATH in plain terms, so that it may be properly classified. Exact statement of OCCUPATION is very important. See instructions on back of certificate.
V. S. No. 1
If more blanks are needed, address State Registrar, 16 W. Saratoga St., Balto., Requesting V. S. No. 1.

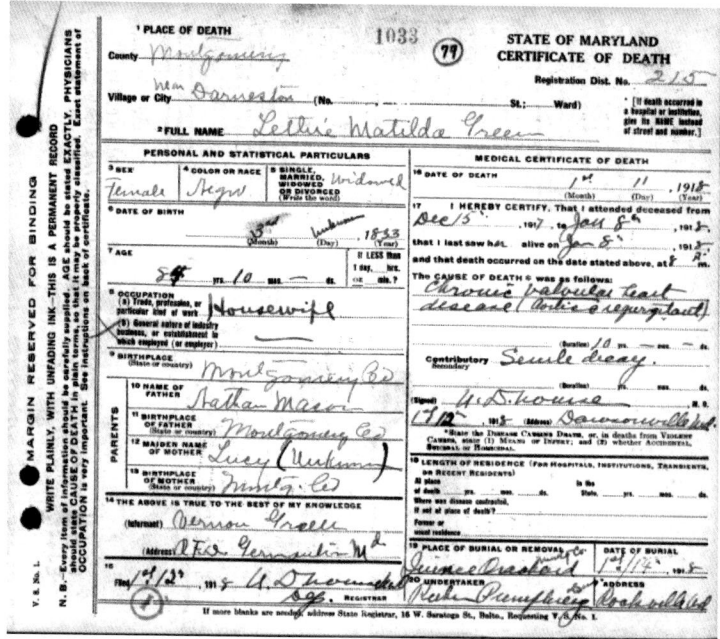

L. Matilda Mason Green certificate of death, 1918

Pleasant View Sunday School class

Ida Pearl Green, Ada Pauline Howard, and Emma Jackson

Jason Green, Ida Pearl Green, and Rev. Gerard Green in the Jordan River

Green family home on Fellowship Lane (snowstorm)

Trustees outside the Quince Orchard Colored School

Grandma Green and President Obama

Ida Pearl Green
and Jason Green at
the premiere of
Finding Fellowship

30 years of Avon calling

Sales reps like Ida Green now visit offices

By LLOYD BATZLER
Journal writer

Ike was in the White House.

The United States fired its first satellite into orbit.

Jet service began between Miami and the Big Apple.

And Ida Pearl Green of Gaithersburg started ringing doorbells.

"Avon calling."

The year was 1958.

"I've been around so long most people call me 'Miss Avon,'" said Green, marking her 30th year as a sales representative for the world's largest cosmetics, fragrance and fashion jewelry company.

Green is one of 1.5 million Avon salespeople in the world and one of about 80 on the East Coast with two decades on the job.

Things have changed so much," said Green, sitting in the living room of her Quince Orchard Road home, which sports a red-and-black Avon welcome mat at the front door and a shiny "HAPPY BIRTHDAY" banner over the fireplace as a reminder of her 70th birthday party last month.

"Now with the higher cost of living, women are at work," she said. "People are spending much more on makeup because women are working.

Avon, a multibillion-dollar corporation that also operates a health-care division, saw the trend and adapted.

"Five years ago, we formally recognized that we had to take those products not only to the home but to the workplace," said Nancy Drumsheller, Avon's regional consumer affairs manager based in Newark, Del. "Five years ago we were still very much locked into the traditional door-to-door home sales."

The beauty group division of the Avon Corp. had sales of $2.2 billion last year. Makeup, skin care products and jewelry are best sellers among the line of 600 products available only from its independent salespeople.

Two years ago, 80 percent of Avon's sales were in the home. Last year, 75 percent of sales were made in homes. Sales have shown a corresponding increase in offices.

There has been a big demographic change in the marketplace with women entering the work force," said Diane L. Mustain, an analyst who follows the cosmetics industry for Chicago-based Duff & Phelps brokerage. "Avon has adapted fairly well.

"They had some difficult years but since 1985 I've seen a turnaround," Mustain said. "Current management is a little more realistic about the sales force.

"They've changed the commission structure. It used to be a flat 40 percent . . . now it's on a sliding scale of 35 to 50 percent to prompt people to sell more, to give them some incentives," Mustain said.

"They've tried to slow the turnover rate because it gets expensive to train people and then lose them," she said.

Avon calculates the average representative earns $10 to $15 an hour.

Like many private corporations, Green declined to disclose her income.

"You are, in effect, your own boss," Drumsheller said. "The earnings are basically unlimited."

The company rewards top producers with bonuses, such as vacations and cars. In her 30 years, Green has received living room furniture, a refrigerator, washer and dryer, organ and record player.

Avon's work to keep pace with a changing society are clear to Green.

"When I first started selling, you got your deliveries every three weeks, and now they're every other week," she said. "There has been so much change in the product line. They're selling jewelry now.

"When I started, cosmetics were geared more toward white skin, now we have products that are for all skin color."

Green bought an answering machine to track telephone calls from customers.

"We have men representatives now, too," she said.

"They've made some changes in marketing. There is much more of a department-store look to their cosmetics," added Mustain, who has watched Avon for five years. "But they've tried to stick to their basic one-to-one selling technique.

And it's Green's personal touch polished over the years, that abet her customers like.

"You have to give dependable service, you have to have a pleasant disposition and you have to use the products yourself before you can sell it."

Three decades of award-winning sales for Avon have given Ida Pearl Green more than just a slew of trophies. She also has won furniture, a washer and dryer, an organ and a refrigerator.

Bill Wood/Journal

Ida Pearl Green
celebrates thirty
years of Avon

Fairhaven Mosaic of the churches

The Green family (Rev. Gerard "Gerry," Kisha, Rita, Jason, and Maya)

in his direction. Sensing their interest, he found space on the other side of the room rather than be drafted into the work.

The Green family had clearly been discussing, or disagreeing over, the future of the church in the short mile-long car ride from their home. Ida Pearl, a few weeks shy of her fiftieth birthday, was well put together and hid her mixture of black and red hair under a trendy beret. Her face meant business and was devoid of her typical piercing smile. Pearl's husband, Gerard, was ruggedly handsome, with a movie star's smile and eye twinkle, but articulating his feelings was never his strong suit. You always knew how Gerard felt; it just wasn't always expressed clearly with words. Sometimes with actions. Sometimes with silence. Sometimes with closed doors. Pearl and Gerard, Sr., disagreed about the fate of Pleasant View.

Perhaps most seventeen-year-olds would steer clear of a church dinner that also involved a parental disagreement, but Junior "Peachy" Green, a nickname he got at birth because his whole body was covered in peach fuzz, was one of the few youngsters present that evening. As president of the Methodist Youth Fellowship, he felt he had an official duty to be present. Plus, with his pending departure to Mount Union College he felt particularly liberated to wade into adult matters, so long as those matters didn't land him seeding a cornfield; he'd been tricked before.

Most others had not yet made up their mind as to the appropriate path forward. Frankly, most did not even fully appreciate the options or the gravity of the moment. The church finances were a topic somewhat confined to the updates in the weekly treasurer's report. The balance in the account had never been overflowing anyway—the annual budget was barely

$6,000—so the current situation did not feel particularly dire until Melvin announced the church would not be able to pay its apportionment dues, the funds the church was required to pay back to the Methodist Conference, unless something changed. Halting small talk continued to fill the room, a thin veil over the congregants' uncertainty as the significance of the moment settled in.

People beginning to eat was the only part of the evening that was going to plan. Pastor Harton, a twenty-six-year-old white pastor fresh out of Wesley Seminary, paced the room, shaking hands and checking his watch. He had previously been pastoring the two nearby white congregations, McDonald Chapel and Hunting Hill, each a mile from Pleasant View in either direction. Until recently, Pleasant View had been led by Pastor Edwards, who commuted from the far side of Gaithersburg. Harton had convinced him to let him take on Pleasant View as well, citing the proximity of the three churches. At the time, it wasn't clear whether Harton had ulterior motivations beyond convenience for bringing all three churches under his leadership.

Pastor Harton had invited a guest speaker, an expert on church mergers, to come and talk to the congregants of Pleasant View.

He was late.

Pastor Harton quietly slipped out of the room to his car to check the radio and see if something had happened to the speaker's bus, which was supposed to be traversing the thirty-mile northwesterly route from the city to rural Quince Orchard. Perhaps the rain had caused an accident, or the bus had broken down again and was blocking traffic.

Harton fiddled with the radio dials trying to get a signal. As the reporter's voice bellowed over the AM radio speaker, Pastor Harton got his answer about the delays. His head dropped into his hands. He sat alone in his car for longer than he cared to admit, then he collected himself and made his way back across the gravel parking lot into the hundred-year-old building to deliver the shocking news. At 7:05 P.M., Rev. Dr. Martin Luther King, Jr., had been assassinated on the balcony of the Lorraine Motel in Memphis, Tennessee.

Gasps, disbelief, then wailing sobs filled the room. Willie Ridgley was a Darnestown native and member of Pleasant View church who had attended school at the Quince Orchard Colored School as a young man and could still picture the hand-me-down books he had received in the same building with "nigger" and "coon" scrawled across the pages. As he heard the devastating news, the only solace he could find was in knowing the Pleasant View community was hearing the news together and could continue to lean on each other.

Pastor Harton tried to calm his congregants by beckoning each outside into a prayer circle around the flagpole. Old and young joined hands and shuffled into the unusually warm April country air, punctuated by a steady light rain adorning their heads like baptismal sacrament. As the ping of rope against its pole kept time on Pastor Harton's prayer, Peachy could not keep his eyes closed. This moment was too significant, and he needed to open his eyes and be a witness to history.

His gaze found Pastor Harton. Everyone in that circle was Black, except the pastor. And as he prayed, seventeen-year-old Peachy watched a tear trickle down his cheek and was stunned. Here was a white man shedding tears over the death of this

Black man. Perhaps, he thought, Black folk weren't alone in their aspiration for all people to be valued equally. As America mourned and cities burned, Pastor Harton prayed aloud for healing and courage. Healing and courage for the country and for those gathered in the small community of Quince Orchard. For the work he prayed they might do together.

Still stunned by the news, the congregants of Pleasant View slowly collected their things, packing up the remaining dinner items in reused tinfoil, and shuffled out of the building quietly without any further discussion of a merger or the church's future.

Dr. King's assassination derailed any plans for a vote on the evening of April 4, 1968, but his sudden death gave the vote heightened significance. When the topic of merger was finally readdressed, Pleasant View was not alone in the room. This time, members of Pleasant View, McDonald Chapel, and Hunting Hill all gathered in the old McDonald Chapel church building. The two white congregations representing the branches of Methodism that had split over the issue of slavery had been trying their own reconciliation. It was not without its challenges, and it made the members of Pleasant View particularly wary about the prospect of all three congregations coming together.

McDonald Chapel was not foreign to the congregants of Pleasant View, the buildings being less than a mile from each other. The different Christian groups had even started meeting jointly and rotating between the buildings. Folks knew their way around both buildings; their architecture was remarkably similar. And for years preceding, members of each congregation had crossed paths at Donald Snyder's store. Hard to say everyone felt at home but they at least felt some sense of familiarity.

As the congregants walked into McDonald Chapel, most made way to their seats without handshakes or hugs, not even among the respective congregants of each church. Looks and glances darted throughout the sanctuary. Some of the attendees kept their jackets on, perhaps hoping the meeting wouldn't be long. But they had at least shown up. Pastor Harton welcomed his three congregations together and made short work of presenting the resolution and his opinion. He looked out at the hodgepodge mix of worshippers and declared, "Christ and Dr. King would want us to be an example of the Beloved Community. The world needs examples of Black Americans and white Americans living together, working together, and worshipping together."

There was no speechifying that day. It was as if the momentum brought about by Dr. King's assassination had already dictated the outcome, whether each individual congregant wanted it or not. Those who had been loudest in protest prior to Dr. King's death sat with lips pursed while a secret vote was motioned.

It had also been decided that should a merger take place, the members of Pleasant View would simply transfer their membership to the new church. The ownership of the land and buildings at the Pleasant View site would not transfer. They were unwilling to part with the land, the church, the historic school, and, perhaps most meaningfully, the cemetery in which their ancestors rested. Pleasant View had been the center of the Black community for so long, and represented the life cycle of the Black experience in Quince Orchard. Giving up ownership would have meant something far more consequential than simply joining with another church congregation.

The congregants from each of the churches cast their

anonymous votes. The majority had lived through the perilous Jim Crow era. Some had suffered the horrors while some had perpetuated them. The decision before them was layered with questions of identity, family legacy, and religious and moral conviction. For some, in that room, it echoed the unfinished work left in the wake of Dr. King's assassination. It's impossible to know what exactly motivated each person in that moment— grief, hope, duty, hurt, desperation—but the weight of the moment was unmistakable.

Pastor Harton slowly counted the votes and then shared the vote tally with measured joy. "We are one!" A majority of the representatives of the three original Methodist congregations, one Black and two white, had voted to merge.

It's said that on the last day of the Constitutional Convention in 1787, Elizabeth Willing Powel, a wealthy Philadelphia socialite, asked Benjamin Franklin, "What have we got, a republic or a monarchy?" to which Franklin responded, "A republic, if you can keep it." Like those sequestered in a Philadelphia hall tasked with recrafting the American experiment, in 1968, the men and women gathered in the McDonald Chapel hall were the founding fathers and mothers of Quince Orchard, and they had decided on a merged place of worship. If they could keep it.

It was the last Sunday of September, but it was a first. Members of Pleasant View drove to McDonald Chapel to officially attend service. When the pastor acknowledged the presence of the twenty or so Black families gathered in the back of the sanctuary, dressed in their Sunday best, an anonymous voice from the group called out, "We've come to join you." There began the delicate affair of the coming together of the churches, and the legacy of Pleasant View, Hunting Hill, McDonald Chapel, and the community wrapped within their coming together. Like the binding of a republic, it would demand intention, faith, action, and a lot of good fortune.

WHEN GRANDMA GREEN HAD FIRST unraveled the tale of the three churches uniting under one roof, she paused, drawing me into the depth of the moment. But just as the April 4, 1968, meeting had been abruptly interrupted by the gut-wrenching news of Dr. King's assassination, I abruptly interrupted her. Before she could reach the crescendo of her narrative, I blurted out, "They didn't merge, did they?"

She shot me a piercing glare. Exasperated, she said yes, they had. Grandma's annoyance with me gave way to disbelief about my disbelief. "Jason, you've been to the church. It's where you were baptized and practically raised. They all merged and became Fairhaven United Methodist Church."

Grandma was right. I had grown up in Fairhaven. The Phillips, the Grounds, the Johnsons, the Alexanders, the Ridenours, the Taylors, the Prasads, the Peytons, the Youngs, the Farises, just to name a few.

We came from different backgrounds, but we all belonged to each other. We kids were all thick as thieves. We got our hands smacked together, we endured Vacation Bible School, and we would launch ourselves off the swing set and over the puddle after church together. I can still remember choir practice in that sanctuary, when an ember from an overhead stained-glass light fell and burned my forehead as Ms. Ground led us in a round of "This Little Light of Mine."

It had all felt natural. So natural, in fact, that I never considered that Fairhaven had to be built. That people, like Grandma, had had to help make and keep it possible. To me it felt as though it had always just been so.

Now I understood how divided the 1960s were. Protests erupted over civil rights, the Vietnam War, the Democratic National Convention, even the Olympics. Bringing races together wasn't just uncommon, it was radical in a time of racist laws, violent backlash, and intense social upheaval. Dr. King was assassinated while fighting for worker rights and for his vision of the Beloved Community, a place of radical belonging that, as he put it, would require "a qualitative change in our souls as well as a quantitative change in our lives."

I knew that Fairhaven was integrated, but Grandma, Ms. Jackson, Ms. Blair, Ms. Ada Howard, and all the others that worked for this to happen didn't exactly seem like revolutionaries to me.

And even though I was a product of Fairhaven, of its rituals and its community, when Grandma told me how it first came to be, I couldn't see it. Not under those conditions. King had just been murdered. The country was grieving and writhing. I had seen too many examples of people walking away from hard things to imagine a group of everyday folks walking toward one.

The merger may have seemed sudden, but it was years in the making—its first mention as early as 1960—through fits and starts and failed attempts and determined returns to the table. Fairhaven was a choice, something manifested through adversity and sustained with hope.

And what is intentionally created must be intentionally kept.

12

IN THE BOOK OF ACTS IN THE NEW TESTAMENT OF THE BIBLE, Paul, one of Jesus's disciples, is imprisoned for preaching the gospel and is being taken via ship to Rome to stand trial. Along the way, the mariners face harsh weather and rough seas and take refuge at the port of Fair Havens. Paul pleads with the ship captain to stay in port, but the centurion, wanting to recommence the journey after losing so much time in the storm, does not listen to Paul's advice. They quickly cast back out for Rome, and eventually their ship is wrecked.

The name Fairhaven had been proposed years earlier by Rev. Kenneth Carder, the pastor who tended the flock before Rev. Harton, and it proved fitting. Neither their coming together nor their staying together would be particularly smooth sailing, and the new congregation would need safe harbor from the storms outside and within.

Underneath a black-and-white image of Black and white men and women with shovels in their hands, the caption in a

1968 Gaithersburg newspaper reads, "Ground breakings are commonplace but this one deserves particular attention because of Black and white congregations coming together."

When the three congregations decided to merge, they wisely built a new building and took on the name. The two white church buildings, McDonald Chapel and Hunting Hill, were eventually sold to help raise the money to finance the purchase. But the Black congregants of Pleasant View refused to sell their century-old property and transitioned the land, church, and schoolhouse into a private trust. They were prepared to be a part of the new congregation and, at the same time, wanted to ensure the heart of the Black community was preserved.

But even before the walls of Fairhaven were raised, some cracks had started to form. I was not surprised to learn that many of the dissenting members left the church after the merger vote. I was surprised to learn that my grandfather was one of them.

Pleasant View had offered an element of dignity to its congregants that Jim Crow tried to deny. Pleasant View had become central to my grandfather's identity. His grandfather Gary Green had helped acquire the Pleasant View site and construct the schoolhouse and church. Grandpa's parents were dedicated members of Pleasant View, and his father, Vernon, attended the schoolhouse in his youth, as did Grandpa himself. Grandpa served as a trustee and treasurer and held a unique stature in the church, unrecognized in the broader world that often dismissed him on account of his race and his fourth-grade education.

Grandpa had personally constructed the church's desperately needed addition. His labor, tears, and memories were all mixed into Pleasant View's foundation, and the merger for him felt like his very dignity was at risk. Merging meant more than just a new building; it forced folks like my grandfather to grapple with identity.

Though Grandma and my father supported the merger, Grandpa sat it out. He felt the weight of what might be lost. It was his family.

Even those members who stayed a part of the merged congregation discovered that the real work was just beginning.

Identity can be tied to physical spaces like churches and the traditions they hold. Merging meant the loss of place, of memory, of control, of safety, of identity. It meant surrendering some of what was precious for something unknown.

Black and white members of the congregation shared memories about their church homes that were eerily similar. They revered the pew where a matriarch sat. They knew precisely when in the service an uncle would start to nod off. They recounted the contours of the choir loft where someone sang in the junior choir. The divots on the floor where women dug in their high heels for generations after having been moved by the spirit. I never got the opportunity to inspect the floors at McDonald Chapel or Hunting Hill, but the floorboards at Pleasant View were almost worn through. And it seemed everyone had a special Sunday School memory.

And it wasn't just the joyful matters. Black and white members shared the same lamentations, as well. Having to listen as a pastor droned through a sermon with no end in sight. Children fretting about spending too much time in church on Sunday, and Monday, and Wednesday. In these country churches, service wasn't constrained to just Sunday morning; you were gathering back at church for Bible study, Boy Scouts, or a movie outing with the youth group. And funerals. So many funerals for aging members of these aging churches, each service revealing a bit about the person and the community they served.

Churches in Quince Orchard served as more than just a religious center. In both Black and white rural communities, the church took on an oversized role as the center of life—social, religious, and otherwise. It's where dances took place, where movies were watched, where dinners and impromptu graduations were held. Pleasant View would hold their craft bazaar, McDonald Chapel had its annual strawberry festival, and Hunting Hill sold mulch—all at the church.

Still, despite these shared frustrations and joys, the merger alone didn't guarantee spiritual alignment.

The tensions weren't just internal; there were real threats of violence. Willie Ridgley said that the police were called up to Fairhaven when the merger was first announced, because people worried about violence. Folks thought the KKK might try to do something. For weeks members of the congregation, armed with shotguns, took turns keeping watch at the young pastor's house, patrolling his front porch, making sure no one came and shot at him or his young family.

While they didn't riddle his house with holes, they did in his preaching career. White members of the congregation, presumably even some that voted for the merger, were so upset with Pastor Harton's reconciliation urging, and his social interpretation of the gospel, that they demanded that Bishop John Wesley Lord, who oversaw the Conference, remove him. Pastor Harton was removed from his post at Fairhaven, never to pastor another congregation again.

King's assassination on April 4 injected race into what had initially masqueraded as an economic decision. But the goal was never just to merge. The goal was to survive. And it became clear that the true significance lay not in the decision to merge but in every day that followed.

These were churches on the verge of extinction, and up until April 4, racial difference had been seen only as a reason not to merge. It was never considered as the reason *to* merge. Financial necessity, not moral urgency, was the catalyst. After the assassination, however, the question shifted: *What would King do?*

I BELIEVE THERE ARE SPECIAL moments when we glimpse history—when the ephemeral moral arc of the universe comes into focus, and we feel like we can reach out and bend it. These moments are intoxicating and all-encompassing, leading to actions that we might not otherwise attempt. The Civil Rights era was replete with them—boycotting buses for 381 days, crossing a bridge despite the certainty of violence, or even the merging of racially segregated churches. These moments suggest the world as it might be.

But then comes the other hard part. Staying the course when the adrenaline fades.

As Fairhaven sobered, and the emotion of King's assassination dissipated, what was left was a social experiment with no clear road map for success, and not everyone wanted it to succeed.

My grandmother's brother Thompkins was ninety-two years old when we visited his Adams Morgan apartment, a menagerie of lush plants in every corner, to talk about how members had to work with intention to keep the merger afloat. Uncle Thompkins had served in WWII and helped to integrate buses, train cars, and restaurants in Washington, D.C. So it would hurt his heart when, despite all the planning and purposefulness, he would walk into Fairhaven's sanctuary on Sunday morning and still see all the Black congregants gathered on one side and all the white congregants gathered on the other. "But I knew what to do. I trained with the Washington Interracial Workshop. We were integrating restaurants and theaters and places of that sort in D.C." He went on, "There were a handful of us at Fairhaven, white members and Black members, such that when the congregation was segregated, we would go and physically sit in between," he said, darting his finger back and forth in the air to mark the spaces where they might sit.

"Was it awkward? Yes, of course. Can you imagine inserting yourself into a space where you were specifically not wanted? But we had learned that it's hard to hate up close, and people had to get proximate." I wondered if I would have the courage to literally go and sit in between people.

Prior to the merger, Thompkins and his younger brother Melvin had warned the congregants of Pleasant View of their financial unsustainability. As he retold the story, I could see in his eyes the desperation of a child trying to warn a parent of pending danger. Because he had been so vigilant in warning the congregation, I got the sense that he felt an extra sense of obligation to help make sure that the merger worked.

"In 1968, it was very important for the congregation to see me as a Black man singing in the sanctuary choir. It's just as important now." Uncle Thompkins still drives himself on the hour-long northwestern route from his apartment to Fairhaven church at least twice a week—once for choir practice and once for church. "Because we need examples," he continued. "Yes, even we people of faith sometimes need to see it to believe it.

"We started having all the different groups start to meet together. And we just had so much to work through, all differences in how the congregations conducted themselves. You heard what the women's group did, didn't you?" he said, leaning in as if he were going to share a secret. "They decided to rotate their presidency. White one year, Black the next. Now, that wasn't easy. They certainly could have just had a vote and let the chips land where they may, that would have been easier. But there were more white women members, and they knew that wasn't gonna get them where they needed to go."

Integration wasn't just about proximity. It was about power. There was a difference between desegregation and integration. Desegregation was just the mixing of bodies, but integration required pure social equity. Fairhaven was threatening the path of desegregation, but its members were hungry to see if true integration was possible. In my opinion, the miracle of Fairhaven is that people were willing to try.

Homecoming, a Pleasant View tradition, introduced more Black culture into Fairhaven. Grandma made sure I understood. "Not the kind for baseball teams or football teams. We would have a homecoming where we invite all the people who once belonged. And they would come home. We would have sermons and singing and a wonderful time together."

Rev. Glenn Young, one of the line of pastors to shepherd Fairhaven after Pastor Harton, wisely invited the Royal Harmonizers, a local all-Black religious singing quartet, to perform their hits—like "Mean Ol' World," "I've Got My Ticket," and "When He Set Me Free"—during Homecoming Sunday to help bridge the musical chasm that some of the Black members were feeling. But annual injections of the Royal Harmonizers couldn't fully solve the disconnect some Black congregants felt.

Ms. Alma Ridgley, Mr. Willie Ridgley's wife and a member of Pleasant View who had joined Fairhaven, was almost embarrassed to share with me that she didn't feel connected to the music at her new home church when the merger first took place. "It lacked a certain spirit. I wanted to hear hymns that resonated with me and my experience in the church."

Ms. Alma was not alone. Clustered together in Aunt Esther's basement, several Black members of Fairhaven, many of whom were family and lived on and around Fellowship Lane, discussed how they could incorporate more of the Black experience into worship.

"It's not just the hymns," Ms. Alma told those gathered. "It's the feeling that we're not really in the service. We're like guests at someone else's family reunion."

Heads nodded slowly and hummed affirmation.

Then my mother suggested an idea: "What if we started a gospel choir?"

The idea received an enthusiastic response until someone questioned, "Would it be—just us?"

The prospect of an all-Black gospel choir was batted around for a few minutes before Ms. Alma interjected, "It has to be integrated, because I'm not going to just stand up and sing just for white folks." The room exploded with laughter. Through the jokes they decided the gospel choir would indeed be integrated. The inclusion of white members wouldn't diminish the significance of the Black experience, and their presence was necessary for the gospel choir to sustain itself long-term in an integrated congregation.

The first member of the gospel choir outside of the basement conclave was William "Bill" D. Phillips, PhD, a white physicist who had recently moved to the area to work at NIST (National Institute of Standards and Technology) and a native of Camp Hill, Pennsylvania, which he described during his youth as "a small town where the Catholic girl was the diversity." Bill and his wife, Jane, would become close family friends. My parents would serve as godparents to their second child, born just a month before me, and my closest friend those early years.

Bill felt called to see if he could sing gospel just like anyone else. "When I came to Fairhaven, I was hearing a different kind of music that was really drawing me in. What I didn't realize was that the few songs that we were hearing in worship was a pale shadow of the type of music that had been such a part of Pleasant View before the merger."

It wasn't perfect, but it was effort. It was coming back to the table with a solution when it would have been easier to throw up their hands in frustration, and that mattered. Back in Grandma's recovery room, which was quickly becoming my place of sanctuary, I felt like it was restoring us both. I would go hide there after conversations to try to make sense of a history I didn't know was mine.

Against the soft hum of medical equipment, I asked my grandmother, "Keeping this experiment together is so hard. Do you ever just miss what was at Pleasant View?"

She fiddled with her hands, took a slight inhale, and exhaled quickly to make sure I was ready for what she was going
to say. She dropped her hands in her lap with intention. "Pleasant View will always be home, but how we have cooperated
and blended together at Fairhaven, it has been wonderful. If
we were back in those days, I would do the same thing again,
because it's showing the world that with love you can make
things work."

She had such an enviable grasp of her position in the arc
of time and space as she continued, "If we are going to be
called Christians and live in a country that talks about equal
rights and things, then it's the right thing to do. And it's going
to be difficult, and you're going to hit your head against the
wall sometimes, but it's still worth doing. We have had our fair
share of ups and downs inside the church, not to mention all
that has happened outside of the church, yet we continue to be
as strong as the people willing to try."

For Grandma, the merger had always been about more
than just survival. For her it seemed like an exercise in faith.

13

ONE COLD, BLUSTERY CHRISTMAS EVE,[*] THE EVENING QUIET was interrupted by a customer entering Snyder's store requesting a pack of cigarettes. The scene was eerily vacant. As Mr. Snyder turned to collect the item, the customer pulled out his concealed weapon and unleashed a deafening crack. The assailant grabbed the cigarettes and raided the till for a meager $100, then sped off south toward Rockville. Another unwitting customer, oblivious to the horror and just seeking to buy gasoline, pulled into the parking lot. He would later tell the authorities he saw a young man run from the store and get into a 1957 Oldsmobile. The customer entered the store and found Snyder lying dead behind the counter, shot in the back of the head.

* Ms. Ada Howard remembers this as transpiring on Christmas Eve, but there is at least one newspaper report that says it happened on December 23.

"Donald Snyder was my friend. We'd been going to his store for years and years." At this point Ms. Ada's grandson and caretaker Kenny stepped into the living room, promising not to interrupt but unwilling to miss his grandmother retelling the Donald Snyder story.

Ms. Ada continued with a matter-of-fact stoicism perfected by a life on the farm. "The boy who killed him confessed to his mother that he didn't mean to kill him, he thought Snyder was going for his gun. Anyhow, he was dead."

Even as the congregations were approaching the merger, the wheels of change were already underway in the broader community. In the year following his murder, the Snyder store property, which included the ten acres upon which the store sat, was sold to the Quince Orchard development corporation, and the dominoes at that quiet intersection began to fall the way of commercialization.

"It all happened so fast I wondered if the developers were in on it." Despite Ms. Howard's conspiracy suggestion, there was no evidence that any developer had any role in Mr. Snyder's death. But it did all move quickly. Snyder's precious general store was torn down as part of a shopping center development project.

"It left a void, that's all. It left a void." Her age and halting cadence adeptly masked her emotion, but I got the sense that she meant that its loss left a void in more than just Quince Orchard's indelible skyline. Hearing her lament the tragic and swift demise of Donald Snyder and his general store made it clear that she felt for him and what his store represented.

"Growing up we never felt poor," my father proclaimed.

"The land provided all that we needed." We all know what that means—that they were rich in love, fellowship, community, and maybe even land, but lacking in dollars and cents. That sentiment captured Quince Orchard well. For much of its existence, dating back to the late 1700s, Quince Orchard was land rich and money poor. It was a rural community where farms were self-sustaining and though not exclusively Black or exclusively white, it was universally poor by outward appearances. Still, there was a shared appreciation of hard work and a mutual reliance on one another. Dad continued, "You see, your grandfather was a skilled builder, and he might build a barn for someone who in return would repair his tractor." Survival was a team sport, and that familiarity allowed some lines to be blurred in Quince Orchard. But that sense of sameness seemed to be changing.

Quince Orchard had long been farm country, with fields of corn, wheat, and hay stretched between dairy barns and pigpens, but by the 1960s it became exceedingly hard to make a living amid farming industrialization and consolidation. Plus, many in the next generation were less interested in the grind of farm life, while the land beneath their feet was becoming more valuable for developers. Consequently, from the early 1960s through the 1970s, up and down Darnestown Road, and throughout the area, farms went up for sale. In the local newspaper, it seemed like the sale advertisements were simply carbon copies of one another. Land was becoming available.

Even earlier, on June 15, 1961, another big decision had been announced that would affect those land values and the future of Quince Orchard. The National Bureau of Standards (NBS),* the nation's authoritative laboratory for domestic measures and standards, broke ground on an expansive 579-acre campus, ushering in both incredible growth and earning Gaithersburg the designation of "Science Capital of the United States." The new site, located on Quince Orchard Road and bordered by Clopper Road—the very two-lane byway that inspired John Denver's "Take Me Home, Country Roads"—drew other science-related firms to do business in the community as well. In the throes of the nuclear arms race, it's rumored the administration in the nation's capital thought it was wise that specific departments be moved outside of a potential nuclear detonation blast radius.

The doomsday scenario planning pushed agencies outside of D.C. but required they stay close enough to maintain frequent contact with Congress and other government agencies.** That was a theoretical boon to the financial forecast of the local communities. The NBS announcement projected the arrival of three thousand direct employees, which said nothing of the myriad businesses that would be created to support and conduct business with the largest standards and technology organization in the world. People needed land. This put Gaithersburg on the map, and threatened to push its surrounding communities, like Quince Orchard, right off it.

Part of the pitch, as described to me, in recruiting scientists and their families to the Gaithersburg area was the promise of

* In 1988, the National Bureau of Standards was renamed the National Institute of Standards and Technology (NIST).
** "NRHP nomination for U.S. Atomic Energy Commission" (PDF), National Park Service, archived from the original (PDF) on February 3, 2017, retrieved February 5, 2017.

large houses with yards, accessible roads, and neighborhoods that were rapidly being constructed to keep up with the increasing demand. One local builder, in an advertising brochure, described the new community as "set among the hills, with a view of Sugar Loaf Mountain. For country living with in-town convenience, just minutes from Rockville. A perfect merger of the graciousness of yesteryear with the streamlined efficiency of today."*

It's said that change happens gradually except when it happens all at once. Over the ensuing decade, change in Quince Orchard happened all at once: Dairy farms were sold; the population of Quince Orchard and neighboring Gaithersburg doubled, with a housing boom to boot; Donald Snyder's store came down and a commercial development went up; and, of course, the churches had merged. My father left Quince Orchard for college in the summer of 1968, and by the time he got back, he explained, "It was like a completely different community, just like that."

Many of the people that were being recruited weren't farmers or middle-skilled handymen; instead, they were often professionally trained scientists and folks with broader worldviews than the community was used to. So, when all the doctoral degrees and security clearances started showing up, there was some apprehension.

Kenny Johnson, Ada Howard's grandson, didn't grow up in Quince Orchard but would visit his grandparents there reg-

---

* David Danoff, "A History of the Ridgefield Neighborhood," *Darnestown Civic*, November 2023, https://darnestowncivic.org/wp-content/uploads/2023/12/A-History-of-the-Ridgefield-Neighborhood.pdf.

ularly. And Quince Orchard, McDonald Chapel in particular, was the first real sense of community that he'd known. Because he grew up with so many members of his family attending the church, even those members that weren't family just felt like extended family.

"One Sunday, I was up visiting my grandmother, but I snuck out of church, you know, to go over and grab some candy," Kenny said, gesturing and pointing out the window as if Synder's store were still standing just a few blocks away. "I ran into a woman I didn't know. I talked to everybody and knew everybody, but I didn't know her, so I spoke. She was new, and she asked me where I was from. And I told her my family was from Quince Orchard. And you know what she said? She had the nerve to say, 'I didn't think there was anything here before but cows and land.' I laughed, you know, but felt like she'd punched me right in the stomach."

Gesturing back toward his grandmother, Ms. Howard, perched in her reclining chair, he continued, "I came back and told my grandmother what she said. My grandmother mumbled, 'They just don't know.'"

The confluence of relatively cheap land and the influx of job opportunities in the late '60s and '70s brought new residents to the area and put pressure on the community's infrastructure. Roads were widened, streets were paved, and new townhouses pushed density even further. Safeway and High's, a grocery and convenience store, moved into the main intersection. And as developments surged, many of the improvements promised to Upcounty residents—like those in Quince Orchard—were slow to materialize.

Education, in particular, became a stress point. The rapid

population changes strained the area's existing schools, and the population growth warranted a new high school, which took years to approve and build. Finally, in the eighties, the school board called a meeting to discuss the development plan and the school's name. The debate over what to name the new school revealed deeper tensions. Some parents were pushing for the name Potomac Valley*—a nod to the affluent zip code more than ten miles southeast. The name suggested aspiration, but for many in Quince Orchard, it felt like an attempt to signal something the community was not.

The shopping center that replaced Donald Snyder's general store, which was originally called the Quince Orchard Shopping Center, was renamed the Potomac Valley Shopping Center, likely in anticipation of the coming transition. But folks underestimated the fight in the Quince Orchard old guard.

When the county school board organized an evening community meeting at Ridgeview, the local junior high school, to discuss the proposed high school name, Grandma Green, Virginia Blair, Alma Ridgley, and Ada Howard were all present. They seemed undeterred by the concerns of fellow church members about getting too involved in the happenings of the rapidly changing community.

Ms. Alma had picked up Grandma on her way down Darnestown Road. As they pulled into the parking lot, she gasped. The lot was full! She hadn't thought many people

---

* The people I interviewed independently recalled the proposed alternate name for the high school to have been Potomac Valley. However, a *Washington Post* article from 1987 suggests that the proposed name was Potomac Falls. "School Board Actions," *The Washington Post*, November 26, 1987, P.M4.

would care what the school was named. Happy to see Ms. Virginia and Ms. Ada, they squeezed in with them at one of the same tables that my buddies and I would likely occupy years later when we attended Ridgeview.

It's alleged that the school board was prepared to vote for Potomac Valley as the school's new name, but my grandmother and the other community members who had been in the area for generations protested. One by one they raised their voices to let their perspective be heard. Grandma and the other women felt no connection to Potomac. To them, "Potomac Valley" felt fabricated. As Ms. Alma declared, "If a high school was going to be built in the heart of Quince Orchard, we were going to make sure it was called Quince Orchard High School. That's how I know protest can really work!"

Those who were pushing for the Potomac name may not have expected such pushback, and really didn't have any reason to encourage the community to call the new school Potomac Valley High other than Potomac plus Seneca Valley equals recipe for success. The new name was defeated, and the board went forward with the community's choice—Quince Orchard High School. Ada Howard said, "Of course I voted for Quince Orchard, because I didn't want Quince Orchard to die." Grandma said that she showed up because she was thinking about her future grandchildren and great-grandchildren. Like Ms. Ada, her thinking about the future was a way of protecting the past to give us something to hold on to.

And she was right. I didn't know Quince Orchard the place, but I knew Quince Orchard the name, because of their work, and that was enough to start following the breadcrumbs they'd left behind.

Quince Orchard High School wasn't just named after a road. It was named for memories, for traditions, for sacrifice, and for community—and in many respects it is now the legacy of all those things.

The brain remembers, but forgetting is one of its gifts, too. Our evolutionary biology is based on forgetting,* and when landscapes come down or change, it's easy for our brains to forget and replace what was there before. It's how we survive. And it's part of why we name things certain ways, because we hang our memories on our buildings and infuse our stories into spaces. When our minds can't leave traces, we leave ourselves markers to remember the essence of "us." It requires a delicate dance between nostalgia and progress, between transformation and preservation; evolving enough to be current yet preserving enough to maintain our sense of self.

Donald Snyder's sudden death was a catalytic spark that ignited a wave of change in Quince Orchard. His old country general store was sold and replaced by a sleek new shopping center. The churches that had been the hallmark of Quince Orchard had merged into one, and plans were in motion for McDonald Chapel and Hunting Hill to be torn down. Just down the road a major federal agency was drawing thousands of people. A new school was needed just to keep up with the influx. Dairy farms gave way to cul-de-sacs. And as more neighbors arrived, folks that didn't know the land, the culture, or the history, an unease started to surface that soon "they" might outnumber "us." Change threatened everything.

* Corinne Purtill, "The New Science of Forgetting," *Time*, April 28, 2022, https://time.com/6171190/new-science-of-forgetting/.

14

I KNOCKED, THEN PUSHED MY SHOULDER INTO GRANDMA'S door, opening before there was an answer and announcing my arrival with a "Hello, hello."

"Here comes Mr. J. Well, you don't stay in one place for long, let me tell you!" It was my grandmother's youngest sister, my aunt Esther, welcoming me into the room. I had missed my Tuesday time with Grandma because I had an important client meeting for a company I'd recently started with a political mentor focused on connecting people to the skills and opportunities that make communities work. I didn't realize when Grandma told me to just come up on Wednesday that I would be crashing Aunt Esther's Wednesday window.

"We're in here!" Grandma chimed in. We all chuckled because there was only one room for them to be in. I wondered if this was a setup.

We had dropped the "Great" from all of Grandma's siblings' "Great-Aunt" and "Great-Uncle" titles, but because she was two decades younger than Grandma, coupled with the fact that she had lived just up the road from us—Esther truly did feel like more of an aunt than a great-aunt growing up.

It didn't happen often, but I remember one night when I was left in Aunt Esther's care at a gospel choir concert. One woman from another church asked if we went to Fairhaven. When Aunt Esther said yes, the woman asked, "You attend that white church?" Without missing a beat, Aunt Esther smiled and said, "Yes, and you should come visit us at that white church." She was calm and collected, unbothered and sure of herself in a way that left an impression. And it was Aunt Esther and Uncle Curt who came to collect Kisha, Maya, and me when Mom and Dad got in a car accident, reassuring us that everything would be okay.

There were several plots of land that folks owned down at the end of Fellowship Lane, but there were only three property owners who had built houses there—my parents, the Bell/Talleys, and Aunt Esther. When they paved Fellowship Lane, right at the end they added in a cul-de-sac, and then two arteries forked from it. The Talleys were the only house on the right artery. My parents were the first house on the left artery. Aunt Esther's house was another fifty meters up the path. To the degree we had next-door neighbors, back there in the woods, Aunt Esther and Uncle Curt were it.

They had a beautiful brick home, with a large patio that flowed into a big flat backyard. For years, she and Uncle Curt had hosted the family reunion in their backyard. We even surprised my parents one year and had their twenty-fifth wedding anniversary there. During those snowstorms it was often Aunt Esther's silver Volvo that we were working hard to shovel a path for so she could make her way up the hill and off to wherever she needed to be.

They were a big part of our lives growing up, so much so that Mom and Dad had asked them to be Kisha's godparents. Uncle Curt was often down at the house helping Dad with some yard work, or vice versa. And Kisha and I knew Aunt Esther's routine so well that we would hide in the woods and throw a fake snake into the middle of the road when she was coming, just to scare her.

I walked over and gave Grandma a squeeze and a kiss and before crossing the tight room to give Aunt Esther a kiss on the cheek, she clasped the back of her hat to make sure our embrace didn't knock it off. I hope I was cordial. I hadn't felt fully comfortable around my aunt Esther since the lawsuit. I had blamed her for some of the changes in the family.

We used to have all kinds of family gatherings for every holiday. One family member would host Easter, while someone else would host Thanksgiving or Memorial Day, the family reunion or Christmas. I particularly enjoyed the pre-Christmas dinner that Grandma and Grandpa Green would have at their house.

On the first Saturday of December, Grandma and Grandpa hosted their children and all their children's children in their little house at the top of our hill to initiate the Christmas season. The gathering was almost better than Christmas itself, because everyone was together, we ate delicious food, we got money. And we didn't have to worry about giving other people gifts. What could be better?

Grandma and Grandpa Green's house wasn't particularly large but operated like one of those clown cars; somehow a seat and a table setting could always magically appear for one more person.

Those early December dinners had an easy, familiar routine to them. Arrive around 3 P.M. Navigate to the back porch, which that late in the year would have been transformed into a gauntlet of Grandma Green's holiday Avon orders, filled with lotions, creams, and other sweet-smelling items. It took me years to understand that the reason I always received deodorant, soap on a rope, or cologne as gifts from my grandmother had more to do with her being an Avon lady and less to do with some persistent body odor I assumed I had.

It probably would have been safer to welcome guests through the front door, but no one ever came to my grandparents' front door except Aunt Helen's lovely husband, Uncle Charles.

We would knock on the back door and then open it, yelling "hello, hello" to announce ourselves. There to welcome us would be all the Christmas dinner smells, roast beef with crisped ends that had sat in its own juices all day to create a light but tasty gravy for the mashed potatoes. I still hunt, often unsuccessfully, for the precise type of ham we would have. It was dry, salty cured ham. I couldn't eat too much of it at once, but it was the kind that I could keep returning to cut slivers off of and fold into a roll or piece of bread. I'd spread jelly on my bread for a ham sandwich; my mother would use mustard. When I was a kid, I thought it was so gross, but now, funnily enough, I've turned into a mustard guy. My grandfather would always pat the ham and gesture a thank you to one of his pigs for making the sacrifice. I'm still not sure if the hams were actually hogs that he had raised, or store-bought hams and he was just making a joke.

Grandpa was a jokester. It was in this kitchen that Grandpa once chastised me for drinking out of a cup the "wrong" way. "Who taught you to drink like that?" he questioned. "You're a Green, not a heathen. Don't put your nose in the cup." Determined to obey, I stretched my mouth wide so that my nose hovered clear of the rim. Then I slowly tipped my head back and proceeded to pour water all over the front of my shirt. Grandpa's laughter grew until it shook his shoulders and threatened to send his false teeth tumbling out.

And then there were Grandma's stewed tomatoes, bright red, simmered with sugar and butter. My younger sister, Maya, loved them, but if I am perfectly honest, I was never much of a stewed tomato guy. Still, like hearing "Silent Night" from the Temptations at my parents' house, it just didn't feel like the holidays until I smelled Grandma's stewed tomatoes on the stove. Even now, I catch a whiff of something similar and I'm back in her kitchen, with the family surrounding me, reminded that something doesn't have to be your favorite to still feel like home.

The meal always seemed disproportionally large juxtaposed with Grandma's small kitchen. The meat dishes would almost overflow the countertops above the hand-carved wooden cabinets, while the stove would be overwhelmed with pots of greens, mashed potatoes, macaroni and cheese, and green beans with small slices of pork simmering for added flavor. And that was just the first steps in the door.

As we walked through the kitchen there was a small office just off to the side. On those first Saturdays, that room was where the sides and salads (and later in the meal, the desserts!) would be placed, and we would all have to shuffle through the small room to serve ourselves buffet style. But on a normal day, while he was still living, that was where I could find Grandpa Green, posted up in that small wood-paneled room tinkering with some doodad, with a vintage black-and-white television playing in the background. Allegedly, my grandparents were the first Black folks in Quince Orchard to buy a television set. Grandma could never say TV; she always pronounced all the letters and syllables.

"Gerard would be in the front room setting up that t-e-l-e-v-i-s-i-o-n set, and my sisters and brothers would come over and huddle around." When they bought their television set however many decades ago, they used it as an opportunity to build community, just as these December dinners did. I think it was probably that same original model TV that still sat in the sitting room.

Past that little office, there was a large room that bore few embellishments. My grandmother's oversized china cabinet took up the entire wall on one side of the room. She opened the cabinet for this occasion; it was like opening day in baseball. When I was really young, if we arrived early while setup was still underway, I would perch myself under the dining table and watch Grandma clean and prepare the good plates. And I would be perfectly positioned to watch Grandpa, Uncle Vernon, and Dad transform the small dining room table by extending it at its sides and inserting one, two, or sometimes even three leaves into it. Seeing how big the table was extended gave me an indication of how many people were going to show up. Would all of Aunt Helen's family be here? Would Kevin and

Tim be there to call me "Chubbs" and quiz me on state capitals? Plus, there were gifts, and did I mention the food? I wondered why anyone would miss this.

Before I was born, the main floor consisted of four rooms, the kitchen, the office, the dining room, and a sitting room/family room, which is where we helped Grandma put up her Christmas tree. But I had always known the house with the addition that Grandpa had built, which included a TV room, a bedroom, and a full bathroom. I'm not sure if he had foresight as he built that bedroom, but that is where he spent the last few years of his life, unable to maneuver the steep stairs up to my grandparents' bedroom. I was also thankful for the addition of the TV room, because that's where, as children waiting for the bus, Kisha and I had watched *My Little Pony* and *Transformers* before elementary school and where Grandma and I would watch *The Price Is Right* before heading off to Asbury.

On the first Saturday in December, the TV room would be transformed into the kids' table space, and serve double duty as the post-dinner nap room. It was so efficient how no one bothered to move the coffee table that sat in the middle of the room. When it was time to eat, we just placed the large folding table right over it. Kisha and I, and eventually our younger sister, Maya, were all staples at the kids' table. So were our older cousins Kevin and Tim, Uncle Howard's boys. The rest of the kids' table seats depended on who showed up any given year; it was like a box of chocolates, you never quite knew who you were going to get.

Holding up the corner of that room was Grandma's six-and-a-half-foot-tall glass case, the hinges of which stuck so bad that it hadn't been opened in decades for fear of breaking the whole thing. Grandma's porcelain Avon doll collection lived inside. Every time Grandma was among the top sellers of Avon, which was quite often, she got a new doll with the year and sales level inscribed on it. Her doll case was full. All the dolls were fashionable in matching suits and well put together, just like Grandma always was, except the dolls were all white.

The house was simple, and it creaked when you walked, but it was sturdy and beautiful in its own way. Porcelain plates inscribed with Avon anniversary years—ten years, fifteen years, thirty years—hung above the doorways, inviting guests in. And just as the dolls and plates were a testament to her determination and success as a businesswoman, two frames hung nearby to reflect her faith. Grandma had these two long before hanging sayings became a thing, the Ten Commandments and the Serenity Prayer. At some point I was made to memorize both but was always drawn a bit more to the Serenity Prayer, perhaps because it doesn't tell me what to do.

God grant me the serenity to accept the things I cannot change,
the courage to change the things I can,
and the wisdom to know the difference.

Grandma's house treated pictures of family members like pieces of fine art and displayed them everywhere. Baby pictures of all her children, as well as their graduation photos, decorated the house. All the grandkids had a spot on the wall, a coffee table, or a place above one of the two chimney mantels.

I loved looking at a black-and-white fiftieth wedding anniversary photo of my grandmother's parents, my great-grandparents,

Samuel and Evelyn Hallman. I would rise up onto my tiptoes and brace my hands against the mantel to see it. I'd never seen Black people in tuxedos and ball gowns before. The picture included everyone who was now attempting to cram into my grandparents' house for dinner, including my dad, who was probably about thirteen years old in the photo, dressed in formal wear. I would slowly scan from left to right, reintroducing myself to the younger versions of the characters I knew. They looked so happy. I always stood a little taller looking at that picture, and not just because I had to get on my tiptoes to see it. It made me proud to be part of the family and hopeful that I would someday get to be a part of an equally special occasion.

Of course, the best part of the evening was when the spotlight shifted to the kids. Grandma Green would don a red Santa hat and perch herself in the TV room. We children instinctively gathered round so she could distribute a miniature animal bank to each of us. These weren't piggy banks, exactly. They were more like gorilla banks with grass hula skirts, the likes of which you might bring back from a Hawaiian vacation. That's not to say they felt cheap. Actually, they felt really solid, like the floorboards of their house.

Sometimes a guest would bring an unexpected child to dinner, a niece or cousin that Grandma hadn't known was coming. But somehow Grandma was always able to manufacture a bank for that child as well.

As soon as the bank was in front of us, it was time to get to work on figuring out how to open it. Over the years, I mastered the art of breaking the bank open along the seam where Grandma had expertly glued it back together the previous year.

When I finally broke the bank open, shiny quarters would cascade over Grandma's carpet. I'd throw quarters in the air and play in my vault like Scrooge McDuck—infinite quarters pouring over my fingers. Then came the stacking. Unlike that Kenny Rogers song, here you did count your money, in front of everyone, mostly so that Grandma could confirm that she had counted the money right. My mother showed me once how to make stacks of four quarters into a dollar. One tutorial was all I needed. I'd make neat rows across and then practice my multiplication tables. The total would amount to about $25 in quarters. Maybe one kid got $26 or another got $23.50, so at the end of the night Grandma would balance the books to make sure we all received the same take. And it didn't even matter if I had to give a dollar back to balance out Kisha or someone else, I could live with that as I was now rich!

Mom passed out coin sleeves to all of us. Now the coin sleeves were more complicated than making piles of four quarters each. I had to open the sleeve and push quarters in while holding the other side with a finger. I found it oddly satisfying to consolidate the lines of quarters into the coin sleeves. Mom would take us to the bank, and we'd exchange those coin sleeves for crisp dollar bills. That became my Christmas shopping money. My senior year of high school, instead of a gorilla full of quarters after the December dinner, my grandmother handed me an envelope. I guess I had been too consumed in my quarter counting to ever notice the envelopes she gave to the adults. The envelope signified my graduation from the children's table.

At some point all those gatherings began to change. Who

got invited to what got a little weird, and some of the celebrations just stopped altogether. Grandma's first Saturday in December lasted longer than others, but eventually that tradition too grew quiet. Maybe it was that all the logistics and organizing had just become too much, as everyone claimed, but I suspect something deeper had shifted.

There had been several plots of land down at the end of Fellowship Lane, adjacent to my parents' house, which hadn't been built on. Most of them were owned by members of the family. Grandma Green's father, Samuel Hallman, was able to purchase enough land to give a plot to each of his children, as well as an additional plot of land in each of their names jointly. These plots lined Fellowship Lane, and we always felt fortunate that they were owned by family. It seemed like insurance against any developer purchasing the land and encroaching upon our house.

Grandpa Hallman likely had great intentions in gifting joint land to his children, but the land became unwieldy. There were differences of opinion among Grandma and her siblings as to what they should do with the land. Grandma felt they should keep the land together and continue to own it as a family, as she believed their father would have wanted. Others felt that since the land was finally becoming valuable they should sell it.

After years of consternation and unsuccessful interventions, my grandmother's siblings decided to sue her over the piece of land that they jointly owned. They took her to the County Circuit Court down in Rockville. There were plenty of folks that supported her—Mom and Dad; Uncle Vernon.

Kisha and I felt so strongly that we wrote a letter to Aunt Esther explaining that we didn't want to see the land sold and developed—but ultimately it was just Grandma's name alone before the judge.

As I understand it, there was no salacious gossip or tawdry family secrets unveiled in the courtroom. The circuit court judge administratively undertook and accomplished what the family couldn't on its own and structured the sale of my grandmother's portion of the joint land to the other joint owners.

I was angry that my grandmother's siblings had sued her. Aunt Esther received the brunt of that anger. She lived next door. She was the youngest. I knew her best. She had always looked out the most. Maybe that made the whole thing feel more personal. But really, underneath the anger, I think I just felt let down. It felt like a break from the very values that Grandma had been reinforcing in our Asbury conversations: family, loyalty, the idea of looking out for one another.

A proud product of the *Goonies* generation, I can't tell you how many times I rummaged through Dad's old books in the hope of finding a treasure map, so I could then gather my crew and set off on an adventure to uncover hidden pirate gold to buy all the land back. Unfortunately, there would be no Hollywood ending this time.

In the years since the sale was finalized, Aunt Esther and the other siblings sold their joint and individual pieces of land— all together—to a developer who came down Fellowship Lane and subdivided the lots. Aunt Esther and Uncle Curt's house, the old Talley house, and much of the woods that had been my childhood playground were demolished. Instead, sixteen single-family homes and eleven townhouses were built where there had once only been three homes. The development even redirected the water, so our little creek dried up. My parents' house was the only original house that remained. It all seemed so selfish. *What about what I wanted?*

I looked over in Aunt Esther's direction as she was adjusting her jacket top, unsure if I was going to take this moment to ask her a question. We had never talked about the land or the lawsuit. I had just sent my unanswered letter. Before the words had been fully formulated in my mind, "May I ask you a question?" broke the silence.

"Of course, Mr. J, what's on your mind? Go right ahead." She got up to fold some of Grandma's things that were sitting on the dresser. They were already folded, so I assumed she was just busying her hands.

"Why did you want to change everything?"

My grandmother looked a little exasperated that I had decided that this was a good time to bring up this matter, and I looked back at her as if to say, *You're the one who invited me.*

My aunt chuckled at my inartful question. "What makes you think I wanted to change everything?" Fortunately, she didn't wait for me to respond. "I assume you're talking about the land down in Quince Orchard? You have to understand, it wasn't that I wanted everything to change, it's just that something had to change."

Aunt Esther continued, "When a piece of land is jointly owned by that many people, each person has their own way of feeling about what to do with it. It's hard to get everybody to agree to one thing. And then you have to come down to another generation who has feelings about the land."

I was looking for a reason to be defensive, and that last line, "come down to another generation," gave me room to feel accosted.

"Well, why shouldn't the next generation have a say in what happens with the land? We grew up there. Those are just as much our memories."

Grandma's eyes revealed she wasn't sure if she needed to referee this or just let the conversation happen. She had come from a generation where you didn't ask questions of those older than you. I was treading on thin ground but was trying to tread respectfully.

"Yes, of course your memories are there. And so are my children's. And so are mine. And so are my parents'. We all have memories, and we didn't sell the land to destroy anyone's memories. When my father gifted us that land, land was cheap. Fortunately, over time, as more people have moved in and there has been more development, the land became more valuable. That's the good news. The bad news was as the value of the land went up, so did the taxes. It just became too hard to keep."

Hmm. I hadn't thought about the taxes per se.

"And no one else actually lived down there," she continued. "So I had my brothers and sisters who weren't living on the property, had no plans to live on the property, and yet were paying increasing property taxes every year. And all the other farms around were selling, why couldn't we? What was I telling them to keep holding on for? Everyone wanted us to keep the land but no one else was ready to buy it."

Feeling some ground slipping away, I said, "But sue *my* grandma." Emphasizing the "my," as if I was just appalled that she would have considered such an action.

Aunt Esther matched my emphasized outrage and said, "You mean *my* sister?"

My grandmother chimed in to calm things, "And it's not that I wanted to force them to keep paying property taxes or anything like that, I have to say that Gerard wasn't thrilled about paying those taxes neither. It's just that the land was part of a vision that Papa had of a Black community where the family could be closely situated with one another. It was an investment."

I liked my great-grandfather's ambition, in part because it felt like he saw into the future and was thinking about me. But Aunt Esther's point was something I hadn't really considered. There were real costs in bringing Grandpa Hallman's vision to life, and no one in the family had the resources to make it a reality amid all the change in Quince Orchard. Grandma couldn't buy the joint land from her siblings. Dad wanted to buy it, but he couldn't afford to buy it all and just let it sit either. If he bought it, he'd have to develop it too. And, since my Goonie treasure hunt hadn't turned up anything yet, I couldn't purchase it either. No one had the capital to build on the land, and so it sat—allowing taxes and frustration to accrue.

Lawsuits are formal and, by definition, draw lines and create sides. The hiring of lawyers, the paying of legal fees, the drafting of filings, all are part of a process that creates winners and losers—and turns families into plaintiffs and defendants. Even when the suit was described as "administrative," there was still plenty of feelings. I imagine childhood slights and school-yard fights that had been carried for years get implicitly incorporated into the filings, taking a toll on the family's cohesion.

Grandma said she stopped hosting the Christmas dinners

because she was getting older and it had become too much to cook all the food and get the house ready to host everyone. Similar reasons were given for the other gatherings that started to change or ended altogether. There was likely some truth there, but I couldn't help wondering if the lawsuit had something to do with it too. However it happened, it felt like something sacred had quietly come undone.

Whatever the reason, it didn't make me miss the gatherings any less. I missed the joy. I missed feeling safe and loved and thought about. I looked forward to that dinner for weeks leading up to it, and then when we were there, time just seemed to slow down. They were my little taste of what it was like when the Quince Orchard community was Black. I hadn't known that Quince Orchard. But I had known this little haven, and now that had been lost too. The end of those family dinners had felt like the last straw in a series of losses; like no one cared about preserving what the ancestors had been trying to build for us.

Then Aunt Esther, remembering the purpose for her visit, turned back to Grandma and asked, "What do you say, Pearl? Are you ready for our lunch?"

I watched them. Aunt Esther helping my grandmother get ready to head to the cafeteria to have lunch together. No pretext or performance. Just two sisters doing what sisters do. It was beautiful to see them interact, and it helped me realize that I had no real claim on that land. Not in the way that they did. Yes, the land had been in our family for some time and its sale was objectively sad. But I was the one that had linked the joy of those family gatherings to the land. I had made the acreage symbolic. Grandpa Hallman wasn't trying to keep the family together to maintain the land; it was about having the land as a means to unite the family. Yet, the very land I'd glorified had become a source of division. I had let it become a wedge.

But there they still were. Sisters. Together.

And watching Aunt Esther, I was reminded that she was the same woman who once watched over me and kept me safe. The same steady, loving presence I had known as a child.

Still, it was hard to shake the feeling that when Black families lost land, they were giving up something more than property. Maybe it shouldn't feel different, but it did. You might gain the dollars, but what is lost?

I thought about asking Aunt Esther if she regretted the decision to sell. But I stopped myself. Whatever her reasons had been, they were hers to carry. I was just beginning to understand my own. Somewhere along the way, I had let the land stand in for more than it should have, identity, memories, even a sense of justice. There is a long and sometimes painful history of Black families and land. What has been held, what's been lost or denied, and what's been taken, often violently. I had let all of that creep in and color my feelings about something I realize I didn't fully understand all the dimensions of and wasn't ever mine to claim.

15

BECAUSE I USED TO WORK FOR PRESIDENT OBAMA, THE principal at Quince Orchard High School would trot me out from time to time to talk to students about civic engagement. In May 2014, she asked me to speak at the National Honor Society induction about service and my time in the Obama administration. On the same stage where years before I was a failed contestant in the Mr. QO Pageant, and performed renditions of "Weird Al" Yankovic's "Amish Paradise," the Village People's "YMCA," and Kris Kross's "Jump" in the school lip-synching contest, I prepared to try to dole out some civic advice. But when I got up, I didn't want to talk about the White House.

I wanted to talk about what I'd been learning.

I told them about the Quince Orchard Colored School. And about how Quince Orchard High School was part of a legacy in the community that dated back to emancipation. I talked about the land patent from the 1700s. I talked about the one-room schoolhouse that had educated the Black students in this community for nearly a hundred years. I finished by asking the students, "If the members of this community fought hard so that the words 'Quince Orchard' hang on the outside of these walls, what are you going to do to make sure the story of Quince Orchard remains?"

Three juniors cornered me afterward. Like me, they had been completely unaware that Quince Orchard had ever been a place or that the high school was named after more than just a road. They wanted to find their own way to preserve the community of Quince Orchard and wanted me to help.

"Mr. Green, we had no idea that this area was full of history. And what you said about community was so cool. We'd like to help you preserve that. Maybe we could bring that back."

I was thrilled they had listened, but I wasn't equipped to be their historian tour guide. I still wasn't sure what I was doing. But I didn't want to dampen their spirits, so I threw out an idea.

"Well, I've been thinking about pulling some of this history into a book. Maybe you guys could help me write the book?" *That was it! I'd come up with a brilliant idea on the spot that would allow them to participate in the project.*

I could see them mulling the idea over, and then they replied in unison, "That sounds like a terrible idea. No, we don't want to help you write a book, but maybe we can think of some other ways to help unearth and save this history. Maybe we could make a film or something."

Well damn.

I still gave them my contact information and told them to

stay in touch. School was about to be out for the summer. I figured they'd lose interest and that would be the end of it.

To my surprise, during the fall semester, they emailed to tell me they'd formed The Quince Orchard Project Club, with about twenty students focused on building community and preserving the history of Quince Orchard. They asked me to join their first club meeting.

Back in my old high school psychology classroom, preserved like a time capsule, I watched as the students trickled in. There were about fifteen kids in the classroom, and at least twelve were white.

Most of them didn't have roots in Quince Orchard. They hadn't grown up on that land or heard these stories at family cookouts. But they chose to carry the story anyway. That moved me more than I expected. They weren't inheriting the history by birthright. They adopted it by choice. And that kind of stewardship felt just as needed. Community begins by choosing to see someone else's story.

Without appreciating it, I had been hoping to find a me in that room—a young Black kid whose family might be connected to this place. But the truth is, I probably wouldn't have been in that room when I was in high school. I hadn't sat with my grandmother to hear this history back then. I understood why a young Black student might hesitate to volunteer to dive into local Black history. It's heavy.

Walking into the Quince Orchard Colored School makes it all real. You feel the warmth of the potbelly stove, see the tight row of desks, feel the burden of what it meant to be called "colored" and schooled apart.

I was a little tense. I hadn't set out to do this. I just wanted to be with my grandmother and collect her stories. But collecting Quince Orchard's story was taking on a life of its own. And I needed help.

Around that time, I was introduced to Dr. Melissa Blair, a history professor at the University of Maryland, Baltimore County (UMBC), who was teaching at the Universities at Shady Grove, not far from Pleasant View. Her students were interested in anthropological storytelling, cultural resilience, and architectural design. I didn't know what those things were, just like I didn't know how to create a program for the high school students who wanted to help. Dr. Blair graciously offered a suggestion: "Don't create something else. Fold the students into the work you're already doing." *Brilliant!* So, instead of resisting, I brought them along and made them part of the work.

Students came with me whenever I visited a community member or did research. Introducing them to elders, and to each other, just became part of the story.

I convinced the Asbury team to let us interview my grandmother out in a larger lounge area where more students could see her. As we talked, other patients listened, readying themselves to share their stories. I'd start the session with a question or two and then turn it over to the students.

They may not have had our roots, but they were carrying our story. And sometimes that's what is needed to keep a legacy alive.

At one point, I turned the camera on the students. I wanted to understand what kept them showing up to tend to a history that wasn't their own. One student laughed and said, "Usually I don't get much out of things—except for dive team. A concussion came out of that. But this—I'm learning how to preserve things, how to connect with people who are such great resources, and how to value what came before."

I laughed with her, glad to see I wasn't the only one getting something from the experience.

During the session, Grandma leaned forward, folded her hands in her lap the way that she does, and shook her head. "You know," she began, "I've always appreciated the family history, but I don't know it as well as others. There are so many names, I can't keep them straight." Actually, that was true; to get to "Jason," Grandma would just run through all the men in the family that were remotely close to me in age. She'd look at me and go, "Gerry, Gerard, Vernon!" but sometimes she would tire herself out and just say, "You know what your name is."

"Vernon, and before him, Cousin Carroll, they're the ones who know the family story in Quince Orchard."

One of the three founding fathers, as the students had started calling themselves, heard my grandmother and voiced what they were all thinking, "Mr. Green? How come we've been doing all this research, but we haven't talked to this guy Vernon who might be holding all the answers?" At least I got them to appreciate primary sources.

I was reluctant to reach out to my uncle Vernon for a few reasons. Chief among them, I wasn't sure which version of him I'd get. Sometimes he was warm, funny, and sentimental. He'd joke about hiring me to dig up roots for his herbal concoctions—at least I think he was joking. He was the uncle that gave me a camping flint or talcum powder for Christmas. Chalk all of it up to quirky Uncle Vern. And he also had the capacity for great sentimentality. For example, when I graduated from high school, he was present, looked me in the eyes, with tears in his, and told me how proud my late grandfather would have been if he were still living. Or, while I was doing some research on Cousin Carroll, who'd since passed, I had come across the most beautiful eulogy that Uncle Vernon had submitted online without telling anyone, attributed to all of us.

But at other times, I'd encounter a completely different uncle. One capable of walking right past me without a glance. No nod. No greeting. Nothing. The shift could be so abrupt, I'd find myself scanning my memory for what I might have done. Uncle Vernon was just a bit unpredictable, and that made me nervous. Especially now.

Still, he'd been the keeper of our family tree, maintaining and building upon a careful archive of names, stories, and details passed down from our cousin Carroll Greene,[*] former curator at the Banneker-Douglas Museum. The students were right. I needed to talk to him, so I scheduled time.

Uncle Vernon lived in the house where he and my father had grown up. Before he died, Grandpa asked him to move back to look after Grandma. When I walked in, I could immediately sense which uncle I was getting. He barely acknowledged me and seemed to have forgotten we had scheduled time to talk.

In the same room where he'd seen me eat many a meal at the children's table, I told him I was working on a community history project. I mentioned the high school students. I thought he might be excited. I thought he might want to share what he'd spent decades preserving. I was wrong.

---

[*] At some point along the way Cousin Carroll changed his last name to Greene.

"Why?" Uncle Vernon dryly replied with a scrunched face full of disdain. "Why do we need to tell the story of our history? Why do they need to poke around our history? The history is already there. It is down there."

He pointed out the window in the direction of Pleasant View, the three-acre site with the colored schoolhouse, church, and cemetery, situated less than a mile east of where we sat. His voice started to rise. "The history is all there. Why do we need *them*?" I assumed he was referring to the students. I shuddered at that word; he didn't even know *them*.

He was agitated and I didn't know why. Exasperated by the exchange, I blurted out, "Do we even know if Great-Great-Grandpa Gary was enslaved?"

Welp, that did it. His shoulders stiffened. His jaw tightened. He rose without a word and walked out of the room.

Stunned, I just let myself out the same way I'd come in.

I sat in my car in the driveway, with a pit in my stomach, confused and angry. And the longer I sat, the angrier I got. *Why wouldn't he want the support? And this "them" bullshit?* I found that repulsive. The idea that we, as the descendants of those who founded Pleasant View, were the only legitimate stewards of this history, while *them*, which seemed to include the students, white folks, and generally anyone that wasn't *of* Quince Orchard, weren't capable of appreciating it? That seemed absurd to me.

I sat in the driveway, fuming. I'd come to offer help. I didn't understand how he could treat this history as private property.

While I was sitting in the driveway talking to myself, trying to understand what had just happened, my uncle got into his car, parked directly next to mine, and drove off. I watched as he reversed onto Quince Orchard Road, idled for a moment, and then was gone.

I started toward Asbury. But as I passed Pleasant View, I saw his car was parked about twenty yards from the front door. After our spat, he'd gone there.

For a split second I considered turning in. But I shrugged off the impulse and kept driving, using my being late for Asbury as my excuse.

I wasn't about to waste a perfectly good moment of frustration. I pulled out my phone and dialed my cousin Melvin. No answer, again. Most folks that Grandma guided me to were happy to sit with me and share their personal story as it related to Quince Orchard, but Cousin Melvin seemed skeptical of me and what I was trying to accomplish, which was impressive because I wasn't even sure yet what I was trying to accomplish.

I'd known Cousin Melvin my whole life. His mother, Ms. Bernice, was first cousins with my grandmother—their mothers were sisters. Melvin was the same age as my dad; they grew up on the same street and even attended the same elementary, middle, and high schools. I saw Melvin at the family reunion every year and at the JuneFest celebration at Pleasant View.

Cousin Melvin casually declined my first request to speak with him. He was polite with it and even had a laugh in his strong tone: "Oh, no, ha. Ha. That's okay. You go ahead and talk with those other folks."

A few months later I asked again. He declined again, and now, no answer. I think he was worried about what I thought of him. There was one major detail that I knew about Melvin growing up. He had decided not to attend Fairhaven after the merger. Like my grandmother and grandfather, his parents had a difference of opinion on the merger. His mother attended Fairhaven. His father did not, and neither did he. After the merger he started attending a different Black church in the community, Poplar Grove Baptist Church.

When I got to Asbury, the gate attendant asked me if everything was alright. I must have been shorter in my answers than usual, and I guess that she could see the stress I was wearing. I decided to treat myself and make my way to the ice scoop for old times' sake and to calm myself down before visiting Grandma. But when I got there and lifted the plastic flap of the ice machine, the scoop was missing.

I sulked down the hall to Grandma. She was all dressed up and looked disappointed when I walked in. "Just you?" Grandma had gotten used to me having students in tow. She liked having the audience and would lean into her stories knowing they were listening. They were prone to pull out their cameras and take pictures and recordings, so she was sure to dress the part.

"Good to see you too, Grandma! Sorry to say, just me."

"You know that's not what Grandma meant. You okay? Looks like someone stole your sunshine."

I didn't mention the fight with her youngest son. I blamed it on Cousin Melvin instead. "He won't talk to me."

Without raising her eyes to mine, Grandma asked me, "Well, why do you want to talk with Melvin?"

I responded, "Because you told me that he would be a good person to talk to."

That was insufficient for Grandma. "Well, I'm flattered." I didn't know Grandma could be sarcastic. She continued, "But

I've told you a lot of people would be good to talk to. I'm sure you haven't reached out to all of them. Why is speaking with Melvin important to you?"

Actually, I had reached out to them all, but nonetheless, I understood her point. Why did I have to break through to Melvin? Was it just because he was the one saying no?

I was working it out in my head and tried to explain to her, "I'm really interested in the story of the three churches merging. I think the decision represents something important about Quince Orchard. And if I'm going to capture the full story, I need to include people like him. People who didn't merge."

Our eyes met. Hers cut, even through her glasses. *People like him?*

"Maybe he would be more willing to talk with you," she said, "if he felt you wanted to get to know him, and not just people like him."

That landed.

She was right. I had not been trying to get to know him or his story. I had been trying to extract something from him. I was approaching him like a case study rather than a cousin, trying to cherry-pick a perspective. I'd unintentionally flattened him into a type.

Eventually, after a few more attempts and, I suspect, an intervening call from Grandma, Cousin Melvin took my call.

"Sure," he said, "we can get together and talk. Why don't you meet me at three A.M. at my place for my jog?"

I blinked on the other side of the phone. "Three? Like, in the morning?"

"Exactly."

I called his bluff. "I'll be there!"

Was this man, some thirty years my senior, trying to punk me with a workout?

I chuckled, but he didn't. This was his interview of me. His test.

I thought to myself: *Get serious.*

He was.

16

MY ALARM WENT OFF—PRAISE THE LORD—BUT I'D barely slept at all, afraid I would sleep through it. I pulled on sneakers and a hoodie and ran out the door. He didn't live far from where he had grown up. Just around the corner and down the street from my grandmother's house. When I pulled into his driveway, Cousin Melvin was outside stretching in the dark, wearing running shorts, running shoes, and a reflective vest. I stepped out of the car prepared to make a joke about the time, but chitchat was clearly not on the agenda.

"I've been waiting for you" rang through the morning air as he took off running. I hadn't even stretched yet and didn't fully know what I was in for. Was this a two-mile jog around the neighborhood or a ten-mile salvo to his days in the military? It quickly became clear that this was a run of milestones, not miles.

Along the way we would talk. Well, Melvin would talk; I mostly tried not to show how winded I was. My collegiate soccer days had been brief and were well in my rearview and he ran this route three to four times a week. Working around the clock at the White House had made me soft. At different points along the way he would pray. Different traditions he had created over the years, perfecting his routine. I was getting a peek into a special morning sojourn (if we could even call this morning?) that he usually did alone.

As I struggled to keep up with my sixty-something-year-old cousin, I realized, as he led me to the stations of his cross, that we were planting the seeds from which trust might grow. We ran past the Travilah Elementary School, which he and Dad had helped integrate, and which Kisha and I would attend years later. Melvin told me the story of how he was called a nigger for the first time in the fifth grade. "It was always in the back of my mind, waiting for it to happen and how would I react when it happened. And true to form, it did happen."

In fifth grade, when the students were at recess playing softball, it was Melvin's turn at bat and one of the other students, a white student, tried to butt in front of him in line. When Melvin refused to give up his spot in line, the student yelled, the beginning was somewhat muffled, but Melvin clearly understood the end: "you nigger!" and the student hit him on the leg with the bat.

There were no *umm*s or pauses as he painted the vivid picture of a well-visited memory some sixty years old. All it took for Melvin to recall it was for me to say, "Tell me about going to school in Quince Orchard," and Cousin Melvin walked me through his memory of fifth grade, detail by detail. I know how being called a nigger sticks with you—the catalogue it creates that rattles around in your mind. And the person who said it—

their face stays with you, frozen in time, seething in anger. "Milton Earl" tumbled out of Cousin Melvin's mouth as though it was a secret that he needed to finally share.

I was surprised to hear how different Melvin's school integration experience was from my father's, despite their being the same age, from the same street and same family in the same class.

To quickly catch my breath, I pretended that I needed to stop and tie my shoelace as we were cresting the hill beside the bales of hay at the Horse Center. Melvin shared that it was in those fields that he and my father had worked for years after school and in the summer. As our pace quickened on the flat road, he laughed about going to Donald Snyder's store for candy as a child and shared almost word for word the same gas-pumping experience there as Ms. Ada Howard. "May he rest in peace." Melvin had a spirituality to him that I didn't expect and held great sentimentality for the things that had touched his life. He said a special prayer as we jogged in front of the land that his parents had rented when he was a boy, remarking how proud he was when he was able to be the first in his family to buy a home. Pride was conveyed with each story, breathing new significance into places that I had previously only rushed by in my car.

We both sort of laughed as we ran past the WELCOME TO NORTH POTOMAC sign that sits at the intersection of Darnestown and Muddy Branch roads. What really bothered me about the whole North Potomac thing wasn't the newness of it, it was the failure to acknowledge the past. One day I put my parents' address into Google Maps, and instead of Gaithersburg popping up, it corrected me that their house was all of a sudden in North Potomac now. According to whom? Just slap a new name on a community and don't address what was there before?

Melvin said what I was thinking better than I could articulate it. "You know, it wouldn't hurt North Potomac at all to acknowledge what Quince Orchard was." I know North Potomac doesn't want to embrace Quince Orchard's small-town poor, but it should wrap its arms all the way around its small-town fellowship and camaraderie.

Melvin is of Quince Orchard. He was born there and grew up on the very roads we were running, even before they were paved. He confessed to driving with a bucket of water in his car so that when he finally got to the paved roads, he could wash all the mud off his car from the roads of Quince Orchard and head along his way. He came from a line of men who got their hands dirty but also cared how they presented. His father drove a dump truck that you could hear coming blocks away. He drove that dump truck to Melvin's graduation, and when he jumped down from the driver's seat, Melvin thought his father had forgotten to wear a suit, seeing him in his dirty work coveralls. But when he looked back, his father had unzipped the coveralls and was walking toward him, proudly, in the suit he had on underneath.

Though at a different time of night than I had ever seen it, and quieter than I had ever experienced it, this route was familiar to me too. Cousin Melvin pointed out Quince Orchard High School as we trotted by, effectively saying "you know that place." Something about being on the jog made me want to share points of significance on the path that I hadn't previously shared either. Like in high school when I ran into the back of a parked car on Darnestown Road, just before the Johnson's Flower Store, days after getting my driver's license.

Of all the places he highlighted along the jog, none had become more familiar to me than Pleasant View. To my surprise, he started to turn in.

He ran up the gravel path and into the bright floodlight on the side of the church building, casting his outline across the schoolhouse. He came to a halt, putting his hands on his knees to catch a breath. A few paces behind him, I was relieved to see he was human. His eyes surveyed the site, taking it all in.

This place had been his introduction to a relationship with God and became the place where that bond was cemented through Sunday School and fellowship with those who fostered feelings of love, visibility, and a sense of home. Melvin looked at me to make sure I fully understood what he was saying and the nuance of it. "I didn't want to go to church with them— with white people. I felt more comfortable with my people. Black people. I didn't feel comfortable going to white churches. It wasn't the same as going to an all-Black church. Pleasant View was my extended family! That felt like it was diluting. Putting the cream in the coffee."

Melvin was raw and vulnerable, and I suspected more honest than most were with me. As he spoke, I reflected on his comments. Of course, attending an integrated church would feel different. It *was* different. But Melvin helped me understand it wasn't just different; it was diametrically opposed to what he knew. One of the few places where Melvin felt safe, seen, and loved was being supplanted to be closer to the very people that made him feel unsafe, unseen, and uncomfortable. And he was expected to just like it.

As we got to the cemetery, he stopped in front of his brother's tombstone and then his parents'. "Why do I come here?" he asked rhetorically. "Because it's peaceful and it reminds me of where I come from and where I'm headed. It allows me to stay in touch with my family's spirit. I know they are still watching over me and caring for me. It's where my family prayed. And where they find eternal rest. It's your blood, son. Part of your DNA is out here. Your great-great-grandparents!" And he pointed at Gary and Matilda Green's shared headstone. "This property is too precious to lose, man!"

Standing at Pleasant View, where, in some ways, both of our journeys had begun and where we knew both of our journeys would end, I saw him in a way I hadn't before. It was like I'd been visited by the ghost of Christmas past, present, and future all in one.

Then, with no goodbye, Cousin Melvin turned and started down the gravel path without me. He turned right when he reached Darnestown Road and jogged off into the early-morning darkness to finish his routine. He left me there to ponder what had just happened and if it was even real.

FEW THINGS FRUSTRATE ME MORE than being asked to give the Black perspective. It boggles my mind that people think the perspective of one Black person must mirror the experiences of another when Black people come from such different places, in different times, influenced by different economic, social, and political factors. But, if I'm being honest, when it came to Dad and Cousin Melvin, I was sort of expecting their experience with integration to be the same. Two Black men, both juniors, of the exact same age, from the same family, growing up on the same street, in the same grade and class. That's about as close as we're likely to get to a scientific control set of circumstances.

I stood in the cemetery pondering just how different Melvin's and Dad's experiences had been. As integration day had approached, Melvin was anxious to see the reaction of distrustful white students. Dad welcomed the familiar faces that he knew from the neighborhood playground joining him in a new, integrated school environment.

When I had pressed Dad, he couldn't call out any specific moments of racial tension beyond his own feelings of being isolated from the community that had raised him. In fact, he told me that he had recently run into one of the white kids that used to live in the neighborhood, a gentleman named Milton Earl.

Milton apparently had lived down at the end of Quince Orchard Road and attended Travilah Elementary School with Dad and Melvin. Dad shared that he and Milton were swapping stories and memories about growing up as kids in Quince Orchard when Milton paused to reflect: "We were lucky. There was just never a negative interaction amongst us kids."

How about that? As my father relayed that harmonious version of Quince Orchard childhood to me, I was stunned. Milton Earl was the same guy who called Cousin Melvin a nigger. Dad hadn't known and couldn't believe it. I wondered if Cousin Melvin had been like me after I was harassed down the hill, and he also hadn't told anyone else the story.

I wondered if Milton Earl really didn't remember. Had he really stood there, casually reminiscing with my father about their childhood—specifically citing the absence of racial conflict—while being the very person who had inflicted a lasting wound? I scratched my head—how many Melvins had been niggers to him? How many Gerards hadn't? What did it even mean for someone to be that person then and this person now? How much forgetting does it take to quiet the conscience?

FOR SOME 150 YEARS THE Pleasant View site was a memorial to the Black community. It is a deeply personal place. For generations, the Black residents of Quince Orchard took it upon themselves to preserve Pleasant View, and even established a trustee board to manage it. Each trustee has a direct connection to the site. Either they or their parents attended the school or the church or both. Even as Pleasant View merged with Hunting Hill and McDonald Chapel, the trustees did all they could to preserve the site. Without their efforts, it simply wouldn't still be on the map.

But as Grandma would say, *What is the goal?*

Is remaining on the map enough?

The trustee board had long been of the mindset that in order to preserve the site, the Black community must keep it to ourselves. The hope is that it will keep the folks that attended the church and the schoolhouse connected to the site and invested in it. The board has persevered by protecting, by shielding, by turning inward.

I wondered if it might be time to preserve by turning outward.

I thought that by introducing a new generation to the Pleasant View story, by letting new people engage the site to build new memories and new relationships, we might try to preserve this site by promoting it broadly. I thought that new residents of the rapidly changing community might be interested if we could show that the history of Quince Orchard and the Pleasant View site had something to do with them—whether past, present, or future. As I learned more, my instinct was to show the community that they had a stake in the survival of Pleasant View, and that they too should be responsible for giving it oxygen. I wanted to convince a new generation that the story of Pleasant View and Quince Orchard was enduring and that the people who built it had them in mind. Pleasant View's story was a Black story, but the effect of its existence reaches far and wide.

I don't think Uncle Vernon appreciated that point. He wasn't worried about creating space for others, in part because I don't think he felt like Pleasant View needed saving. To him, Quince Orchard didn't need to be brought back. It still existed at Pleasant View, preserved in just the form he wanted, present and available whenever he needed it.

Pleasant View had survived for so long due to the efforts of Black people that I needed to really sit with Melvin's comment: Would white participation necessarily dilute things? Was the merger just like adding cream to the coffee? Uncle Vernon saw me as someone who was being reckless with a rare, old diamond. But was it reckless to want to shine up the diamond so that everyone might bask in its reflection and see its worth? Or was it only worth saving for Black folk? Or was it a fear, rooted in history, that if we shined it up too bright, others might claim it as their own, leaving those who had nurtured it without the treasure they'd worked hard to preserve?

I was so tired from our run and from thinking and questioning; when I got back to the house, all I wanted to do was shut off my brain and fall asleep in front of the TV. I flipped through some shows—"programs," as Grandma would call them—and landed on an old classic, *A Few Good Men*, that '90s courtroom drama about military justice and moral ambiguity. Jack Nicholson's Colonel Nathan Jessup was about to take the stand to square off with Tom Cruise's Lt. Daniel Kaffee. I'd always gravitated toward Cruise's character, sharp, clean-cut, driven by justice. But Nicholson's gravelly monologue always captured my attention:

> *We use words like honor, code, loyalty. We use these words as the backbone of a life spent defending something. You use them as a punch line. I have neither the time nor the inclination to explain myself to a man who rises and sleeps under the blanket of the very freedom that I provide and then questions the manner in which I provide it. I would rather you just said thank you and went on your way. Otherwise, I suggest you pick up a weapon and stand a post. Either way, I don't give a damn what you think you're entitled to.*

I'd recited that passage tens if not hundreds of times, trying to perfect Jessup's tone and delivery. But with my conversations with Uncle Vernon and Cousin Melvin weighing on me, I heard Colonel Jessup's words anew. I had been disappointed in how these camps—*us* and *them*—were formed. But as the courtroom scene played out, I realized: It wasn't just the students that had been put in the *them* camp.

I was "them" too. I had gotten to go away and had stayed gone. College. Law school. The campaign. The White House. I'd been chasing degrees and dreams. They had been standing the post. They'd defended the historic Quince Orchard site, protected our legacy against encroaching development and had held the line. They had served as trustees. They had cared for my grandmother. They had preserved our history. They had curated an entire experience and ensured our story had a place in the community.

And now here I was, back and full of questions—feeling entitled to critique the very way they had kept the story alive. Maybe they would've preferred I had just said thank you and gone on my way.

The umpteen times I'd watched *A Few Good Men,* the story was always black-and-white. Colonel Jessup was the villain. No nuance, no sympathy. He had done wrong and deserved his punishment. But this time, sitting in the gray space of my own life, I saw him a bit differently. Jessup was from another time. He was a product of it and had given his best years to navigate and survive by its rules. It had taken his best years and moved on without him. That doesn't make his actions right, but it does make them more understandable.

Before the semester ended, I asked the students to help me locate the original deeds to Pleasant View, dated April 1868. We found them in the archives—beautiful, handwritten documents, full of intention. I thought about all the hands that had touched those deeds. They were like a relay baton passed through time. We printed them and had them framed.

I wrapped the frame carefully and left it for Uncle Vernon. A peace offering of sorts. A quiet way of acknowledging that his work was seen, respected, and appreciated. A thank-you.

17

MELVIN HAD STOOD IN THE PLEASANT VIEW GRAVEYARD and pointed to the tallest tombstone—my great-great-grandparents', Gary and Matilda Green. The encroaching townhouses in the near distance felt like tourists at the White House gate, huddled together, trying to lean over and see the fortune, hope, and promise that the cemetery held, nestled between the church and the schoolhouse.

As the sound of Melvin's sneakers on the gravel faded away, I was alone in the cemetery. It was nearing 4 A.M. It was still except for some foraging deer. No traffic. No voices. Just an occasional chill. It felt hallowed.

Pleasant View was a full-circle kind of place. Generations came here to be educated. They came here for spiritual renewal. And, ultimately, when their journey ended, they came here to rest.

I played in that field as child. Every year at the MayFest

celebration, my dad's older sister (my aunt Helen) and Cousin Bernice (Melvin's mother) would gather us around and prepare us to wrap the maypole. I can't imagine that they knew the pagan fertility origins of the wrapping of ribbons around a tree or a flagpole during spring festivals, something wholly unrelated to our celebration. For it was a ritual of remembrance and joy.

That was my real draw to the annual celebration, more than the opportunity to tour the historic schoolhouse and church buildings, or the tremendous catering services of my aunt Esther and uncle Curt, even beyond the "when I was your age" stories from those who had spent their formative years on this land.

Each child was given a colorful spool of ribbon. One end was tied to the top of the flagpole. We'd pull until we were in a circle, with our ribbons as colorful spokes coming from the flagpole. Aunt Helen would tap every second child to turn the opposite way, and we'd begin our careful walk, weaving the ribbons into a beautiful spiral. A beautiful idea that always devolved into chaos. Pure joy!

I had also stood in that cemetery for my grandfather's funeral. When I was ten, we gathered at Fairhaven for his service. I was proud of myself that I didn't cry at all. Not even at the interment at Pleasant View. But as we started back across the cemetery, about to the point where I was now standing, Cousin David looked down to ask, "Jason, are you doing alright?" and that's when my floodgates opened.

Now, alone in that cemetery, I stood before the headstone for Gary and Matilda. I didn't want them to just be names in

family lore. Before I left, I ran my fingers over their etched letters, tracing their birth and death dates. I wanted to know what
had happened in the middle. I'd filled in details before, but the
truth was, I didn't know their full story.

The story that was told at every family reunion was that
Matilda Mason met Gary Green, an aspiring carpenter, in
Quince Orchard. They fell in love there and built a family with
twelve children.*

It struck me that this had all happened in the mid-1800s,
and yet there was no mention of slavery. Just a casual chance
encounter that turned into love.

I stood there for a long time, not ready to let the moment
go. The stillness felt like magic. I couldn't just walk out of a
moment like that; it felt like I might not find it again. Standing
where others had learned and prayed, gathered and grieved, I
still had questions. What was the true story about Gary and
Matilda? Not the family legend. Not the Disney version. But
the real story.

The more I stood there, the more I realized the conversation I needed to have. I wasn't ready for another round with
Uncle Vernon, so I went to Grandma Green.

"Grandma, were Gary and Matilda slaves?" I asked, sure
of the answer.

"No. Slavery didn't exist in this part of Maryland."

Grandma was so certain that for a hot second, I accepted

---

* Although that is what was repeated at family reunions, the 1900 census
actually lists Matilda Green as head of household, and she is identified
as having given birth to up to fifteen children.

what she said. In part because it was a better answer to hear, and in part because this was my grandmother—trusted matriarch, source of all family information. But then I had to push back. There was most certainly slavery in Maryland.

"Well, Grandma, I'm pretty sure slavery existed in Maryland. For example, Frederick Douglass and Harriet Tubman were enslaved in Maryland."

She quickly retorted, "I said 'in this part of Maryland.'" She had a point; she had said that.

"Yes, Grandma, but I don't think slavery worked that way. I think if the state was a slave state, then the whole state had slavery."

Then she looked straight at me. "Jason, I don't know if my grandparents or my grandparents' parents were slaves or not. You know, I think it was too hard to talk about."

Grandma didn't need me to prove to her that slavery existed in this part of Maryland. She had built a version of our family story that made space for pride and left the uglier truths in the margins. It's the only way I could understand how she had crafted such a narrative to carve out her own family, knowing that slavery existed in Maryland. Grandma had filled in the blank spaces left by her parents', grandparents', and great-grandparents' refusal to talk about enslavement.

Anthony "Tony" Cohen, president of the Menare Foundation, is a legend when it comes to the teaching of the history of American slavery. He once shipped himself "north to freedom" inside a crate on an Amtrak train as a way to investigate the underground railroad; he prepared Oprah Winfrey for her role as Sethe in the iconic film *Beloved*. I had gotten to know Tony years earlier when we served on a local heritage board together.

He possessed a rare gift for pulling together disparate historical facts to paint a comprehensive story.

After my grandmother's response, I solicited Tony's help to trace and expand my family tree. I had come to appreciate how fortunate I was to even know my great-great-grandparents' names, let alone their birth years. Gary Green was born in 1832, and Matilda Mason Green was born in 1833. But still, I had no definitive way to know if they had been enslaved.

Tony invited me out to Button Farm, his living history center in Germantown, Maryland. The farm was part of land owned by the National Park and Planning Commission, and he had restored a house and farm on the property to appear like a functioning slave plantation from the early 1800s. Tony lived there. As we walked the grounds, I felt transported back to plantation times. Tony kept saying that my great-great-grandfather "would have likely managed" this or "been held responsible" for that as he picked up particular tools and described common tasks. I kept correcting him to say that we didn't yet know for sure if my ancestors were enslaved. I knew that in all likelihood they had been, but Grandma's straight-faced denial was still on my mind, fueling a strand of hope that maybe, somehow, my people had been spared.

Sensing my discomfort and trying to mask an eye roll, Tony offered to help me reach a definitive answer. "The Maryland Archives in Annapolis are a wonderful place for us to start," he said.

A few weeks after my visit, Tony's name popped up on my phone. For some reason, I let it ring a few more times. Finally, I answered.

"I was able to do some research, and I think I found some

information that might help you round out your family tree. Why don't we gather your parents, your grandmother, and your sister, and I can share what I found with you."

I'd initially reached out to Tony because I didn't know where to start the search on my own. But now that he'd found something, I wasn't sure I wanted to know anymore. I almost called it off. Finding out could be painful, and Lord knows, I didn't want to cause harm. As long as I didn't know, I could do like my grandmother had already done. I could fill the void with my own narrative.

Because I didn't know exactly what Tony had to share, I didn't know how to explain to my family what the discussion was going to be. So, I didn't. "My friend Tony asked if we could all gather at Mom and Dad's house. It's important" was all I said.

It was imperative that Grandma attend. We negotiated with her doctors to spring her out of Asbury for an afternoon. It wasn't completely unusual for us to take her to lunch in the area and then bring her back. When we took her for the full-day visit to the White House to meet President Obama, every nurse working that day asked if they could be attached to her side. This, obviously, was different. I explained that it was an important family gathering and we'd have her back before long. The nurses didn't seem as interested this time.

When Grandma arrived at the house, she turned to me and asked, "How's our project going?" I liked the idea of us having a project. I guess we were about to see.

Inside, Tony was setting up his presentation with an ominous stack of manila folders under his arm. We situated ourselves in a circle in the living room, Mom and Dad sharing the love seat. Grandma and Uncle Howard (Dad's older brother) settled on the couch. Kisha took the big sitting chair; she was nursing Byron, her second child. I pulled in additional chairs for Tony and myself. We'd invited Uncle Vernon, but he didn't come. I tried to offer general pleasantries, but my focus was fixed on the folders.

Tony brought calm and care to our conversation as he asked my father to present our family tree aloud. Dad began reading the tree, starting with himself.

"My name is Gerard A. Green, Jr., and I'm the son of Ida Pearl (Hallman) (Bell) Green and Gerard A. Green, Sr."

He proceeded up both sides of his tree until he stopped at Gary and Matilda. Dad halted. "That's as far it goes. It sort of ends there." Tony looked at each of us, making sure we understood the significance of what he was saying.

"It is a gift to know as much as you do. Most Black families can't trace their family back three generations. You're able to go back five." Quietly, I wondered whether six was too much to ask for.

Tony passed one manila folder to me and another to my father. He asked Dad to begin reading.

Then, in his counselor voice, which I knew all too well, Dad began. "A Record of Slaves in Montgomery County . . ."

The living room banter stopped, and everyone fell into a hushed silence, all eyes focused on the ruffled papers. I felt sick. As Dad silently perused the sheet, his eyes landed on something—whatever he was supposed to be searching for. He lowered his head, almost in defeat. It was like the air had been knocked out of him. After taking a moment to steady himself, he cleared his throat to reveal to the rest of us, anxiously awaiting the cause of this reaction, what he'd seen.

Name of Owner: John H. Higgins. Name of Slave: Gary Green.
Age 33.
Term of Servitude—for Life.

My mother gasped while my grandmother nodded silently. Tears welled up in my father's eyes. As the records circulated, a chill ran through me. I was thirty-three.

The words hung suspended in the air. I held my breath waiting to hear Dad read the names of Gary's wife and children but was surprised when that didn't come. The story had always been that Gary and Matilda lived in Quince Orchard with their twelve children. But as I looked at this slave census from 1864, I noticed only two enslaved people were owned by John Higgins—Gary Green and Maria Coates. Maybe Matilda was free. I'd heard stories of families where one member was free and the other enslaved. My mind quickly began spinning a story of maybes. My positive bias had Great-Great-Grandmother Matilda somewhere free in Pennsylvania, before Tony pulled out another folder.

He passed it to Kisha. She read aloud, "Slave Record of Montgomery County. Name of Owner: Samuel Higgins. Name of Slave: Matilda Green." And then she read the names and ages of their children. One as young as two years old.

My head just fell into my hands. No words.

When the folder finally reached me and I saw Matilda's name alongside "for Life," I was overwhelmed. Tears blurred my words. A mix of feelings stirred within me, somehow both shame and pride. In holding my great-great-grandmother's record, there was something powerful about seeing her name in print. Even if that print was a slave record. This paper confirmed that she lived beyond the stories we told and didn't tell. She existed even beyond our family reunion book, documented in the annals of history.

My dad can get emotional. It's one of the things that makes him a good pastor and a great father. He's unafraid of authentic feelings. I wasn't surprised that the unveiling of his great-grandfather's slave record brought him to tears. But I was surprised at why. "The tears came because I don't feel lost anymore," he said. "I have a sense of a beginning."

And I guess I did too.

Tony asked me to read the contents of the last manila folder—the 1870 census. Some census worker of the time had gone door-to-door collecting people's name, age, race, occupation, and literacy status, making entries down the page in a gently slanted cursive that reminded me of my mother's handwriting. I read the first full household on the page:

"Green, Gary, 40, Male, Black."

Then, below Gary was "Matilda, Jane, Janet, William, Robert, Alexander, Ernest and Emma."

They were intact as a family.

Gary's profession was listed as farm laborer, Matilda's as keeping house. The document revealed that neither Gary nor Matilda could read or write. They had two other adult Black men living with them as farm laborers.

Two of their children had been born after emancipation, one of whom, listed at two years old, was Gary and Matilda's youngest child yet, Emma.

Emma is my grandmother's grandmother.

Emma gave birth to Evelyn, who in turn gave birth to Ida Pearl.

If the family had been separated on the auction block, Emma would likely have never been born. My line—this story—could have ended there.

I got emotional scanning the 1870 census page and seeing the Green family all together.

Not property. Not scattered.

Free.

Before everyone departed, Tony said that since so much of our time had been spent in reflection on the past, he challenged us to consider our hopes for the next 150 years. Everyone offered something—faith, family, connection—but it was Grandma who took us home:

"Just a few years after enslaved people were emancipated in Maryland, our ancestors helped collect $54 to build a schoolhouse for Black children."

"I still can't believe they did that," I interrupted. As a Washington lawyer, I'd become really good at risk assessments, and this seemed so risky. "There had to be a safer, less conspicuous way to achieve the goal."

Grandma didn't miss a beat. "There was no public education for us in Montgomery County. The children needed a school! And so, Gary and Matilda and those other men and women looked around the community, saw this need, and took action because they were doers and doers do."

So simple, yet so profound. It felt like the gospel as told by Grandma.

18

I T WAS RIGHT BEFORE CHRISTMAS OF 2016 WHEN I GOT THE call. Ms. Ada hadn't been well. At that age you pray for quality of life over quantity. And what an incredible life. A proud mother and grandmother, she spoke so fondly of her time as a teacher, usher, and church leader. She had lived valiantly and worked intentionally to etch her family's name into the Quince Orchard history books, to integrate her church community, and to ensure that the name Quince Orchard itself lived on for future generations.

Seven months after her one hundredth birthday, Ms. Ada Howard was called home.

I had only come to know her late into her life, but because I spent so much time with Ms. Ada in those last years, her grandson, Kenny, bestowed on me the great privilege of being an honorary pallbearer at her homegoing service. The funeral took place at Fairhaven. Of course. Ms. Ada was laid to rest at Forest Oak Cemetery on Route 355, among a smatter-ing of headstones engraved with Howards and Smalls, across from Grace United Methodist Church, the original Methodist Church South in Gaithersburg that had birthed Ms. Howard's beloved McDonald Chapel.

As a bright December sunlight cascaded down and Ms. Ada was laid to rest, I felt thankful for the unexpected opportu-nity to become friends with a hundred-year-old white woman who was the matriarch of a church whose foundation was rooted in slavery. And yet that wasn't even what we had talked about. We talked about her beloved Quince Orchard and its self-sustaining farms, dirt roads, and general store. We talked about how her family had played an early role in shaping Quince Orchard and neighboring Darnestown and how it was important to her that people knew the name Quince Orchard. We talked about how regular folks, Black and white, had built Quince Orchard, and it was up to regular folks to make sure it didn't die.

And, of course, we talked about the unlikely merger. When I had asked Ms. Ada if she supported it, with conviction she had told me, "I worked for it. Young people were running the church now, and we would accept anyone regardless of race, creed, or color."

Death makes me think about death. And as I watched Ms. Howard's loved ones say their tearful goodbyes, I remembered so many others with whom I'd gotten to sit and bear witness to their lives before they were called home. Many more were called home long before I ever got the chance to sit with them, but I heard their stories through the words, reflections, and tears of those I did. Whenever someone that we had interviewed passed away, I would share my notes and their recording with their loved ones. Rarely did we get to spend much more than an hour or two with a Quince Orchard elder, yet our recordings were often the most comprehensive final memento a family had.

As I sat at Ms. Ada Pauline's homegoing service, I thought about her Quince Orchard "twin," Ida Pearl.

Every time I'd walked into Grandma's room at Asbury, I would ask the same question to gauge how our session was going to go. "Are we having a good day?" Some days she'd just say yes or no. But some days she'd give me a little sass and say something like, "You mean we *me* or we *we?*"

The best days were when she was thinking not just days but weeks and months ahead. When Grandma would end our time with something like, "When you head home, could you do me a favor and go buy some flowers and take them by the house?" Take them by the house meant plant them. "I'd like flowers when I go home. Be sure to buy perennials, so they'll bloom every year."

Other days she'd complain that her leg was giving her unbearable pain. I'd walk into the room and see her bent over, rubbing her leg from the knee to the ankle. She had stopped hiding her pain from me and pretending she was always fine. I considered that progress. On those days, I wished that she would just let the doctors amputate her leg, get fit for a prosthetic, and just be on with it—but it wasn't my place.

I was there to spend time with her and collect her stories, and I understood my broader assignment. I couldn't take away the pain in her leg or the weight on her spirit, but I could shift the mood. A good story, a shared memory, even a bad joke might help her feel lighter, even if only for a moment. How could we make the suffering smaller by making the joy louder?

One morning when I pushed my shoulder through her door to ask if it was going to be a good day, I stopped as soon as I crossed the threshold. I didn't have to ask a thing; it was obvious. Grandma was beaming. Her radiant twinkle told me this was no ordinary day. It was too early in the morning for her to have had any other visitors, so I was slightly confused as to what could have brightened her day so.

"It sure is a beautiful day today, Grandma, isn't it?"

"Oh yes, it is," she chirped back with enviable energy.

"The sun is shining outside, Grandma. How you do?" as Miss Emma would say.

"Oh, I'm just wonderful," she proclaimed.

"You're always wonderful, Grandma," I quipped. "Anything new?"

Grandma looked around like she had another secret to share. And then she leaned in and said, "Welllll," all long and drawn out, "I'm going home." Accenting her words with her hands tapping her lap.

I stopped and stared. "You are? That's fantastic news, Grandma! The doctors told you that you were cleared to go home?" I immediately radiated too.

"Well, not exactly," she said.

"Oh? Okay, well, what exactly?" I responded gently, not trying to kill her vibe.

"I had a dream."

The fact that she was holding on to a dream as her affirmation that she was going home actually didn't worry me in the slightest. I didn't take it as literal truth, but then again, my grandmother had a pretty remarkable track record when it came to dreams turning into reality.

I asked her to give me the details. According to the dream, first, a new doctor was going to start giving her a new treatment on her foot. And, last but certainly not least, the new treatment from the new doctor was going to work and she would be able to go home. Bingo bango.

Now, having heard the dream, and knowing my grandmother's dream manifestation history, I should have been over the moon, but my logical mind restrained me—*and* this particular story sounded oddly familiar. I thought that perhaps my grandmother, whether knowingly or not, might've been recycling a story from her childhood.

When my grandmother was a young girl, she'd had trouble with her foot. It was so bad that she was admitted to Children's Hospital in Washington, D.C., where doctors after evaluation and consultation decided that they needed to amputate. Grandma could never quite pinpoint what the prognosis had been. The doctors were on high alert for polio after cases had spiked in 1916. At some point, polio was ruled out, but her terrible symptoms were persistent and debilitating.

After much deliberation, Grandma's parents decided to accept the doctor's recommendation to amputate her foot. They signed the paperwork on a Sunday for the Monday operation. That same Monday morning, while Grandma was being prepared for surgery, a new nurse stumbled into her room and saw her chart. She had just been transferred from a different hospital where one of her patients was suffering from something that seemed similar, and she had started an innovative treatment that had been effective.

The nurse begged the doctors to allow her to try the new treatment on Grandma's foot before they amputated. The nurse was persistent; so persistent that Ida Pearl's parents joined the chorus. Eventually, the doctors relented. This is one of those scenarios where being a little Black girl was to Grandma's advantage. It was no skin off the doctors' back if she didn't get better. Sure, they said, let the new nurse work with her.

The nurse spent days with my grandmother, soaking and treating her foot back to health. A few weeks later Ida Pearl was able to walk out of Children's Hospital, foot still attached. Grandma considered that nurse to be one of the angels that had touched her life. I'd heard the story so many times that I could see the nurse—a vivid picture in my mind's eye—in her starched white nurse outfit, smiling over a young Ida Pearl.

As a lawyer, one thing I can do is spot a fact pattern, and there were a lot of parallels between Grandma's new dream and the miracle story from her childhood. Too many, if you asked me. I thought that perhaps this time, instead of it being a prophetic dream, it was just her subconscious mind at work. By this point, I'd learned my lesson about challenging my grandmother, so I didn't want to tell her that she was wrong. I just thought I'd elicit enough details from the newest dream that she might come to her own conclusion that she was simply remembering.

My continuous barrage of leading questions didn't seem to mute Grandma's excitement about her dream one bit.

When I finally asked, "Who is the new doctor?" she responded, "Well, that's the best part. We already know them!"

"We do?" Now I was completely sucked in. I took the bait. "Who is it?"

"Kisha! Your sister!"

Grandma's face illuminated genuine joy, and she flashed her beautiful smile. She was inviting me to affirm her excitement. I knew better than to dim her light. She had hope, again. There really is no age limit on hope's ability to transform. As Grandma beamed from her dream high, I slipped into the hallway and pulled out my cell to give Kisha a heads-up.

I told my sister a truncated version of the story Grandma had just shared with me: "She'd had a dream that a doctor started a new treatment on her foot and that she was cured and got to go home." Lastly, and most importantly, I shared that, according to Grandma, "The new doctor in her dream is . . . you!"

With all the excitement of someone who had gotten called for jury duty, Kisha responded, "Yeah, I heard." Apparently, the first thing Grandma had done when she woke up was call Kisha to share her dream. "What am I gonna do? I'm no foot doctor!"

What could she do?

Soon Kisha, a family medicine physician, was supplementing Grandma's medical care. She studied Grandma's ailments, pored over charts, read up on case studies, and initiated every remedy she could find—topical treatments, supplements, circulation therapies. None seemed to work.

Until one did.

True to my grandmother's dream, her new doctor, my sister, implemented a combination of treatments, and slowly, things began to improve. Grandma's circulation got better. And it continued to get better. So much so that she was told she would be able to go home—with her leg intact. She was going to get to leave the building where she had sat over the years and loved on many individuals that never got to go home. My grandmother had watched her own mother transition to the afterlife at Asbury. But Grandma was going to go home. Just like the dream said. Simple as that.

Kisha climbed the ranks from granddaughter to grand angel.

Ever since September 11, I haven't been able to trust a clear blue sky, but the day Grandma was set to leave Asbury started to reclaim them for me. I walked through the front doors beneath those cloudless skies, carrying a bit of residual doubt that was immediately lifted when I got to her room. Grandma was already all packed, sitting by the door in her wheelchair. She was out of her bed, fully dressed in a maroon pantsuit that matched the rouge on her cheeks. She was radiant. Her room at Asbury, once a place of uncertainty, was full of hope and excitement.

Dad came up to the room to get us. I expected Grandma to look nostalgically around her room and perhaps reflect on the time spent there. Nope. When Dad walked in, Grandma said, "We've been waiting for you."

Grandma had never been one for prolonged goodbyes. During our visits, she always placed more emphasis on the warmth of hellos. The goodbyes were often brisk, ending with a casual "bye now." It's as if she never wanted to make a fuss about parting, sensing that one day, inevitably, one of those goodbyes would be her last.

Grandma had her satchel sitting on her lap, and I threw the rest of her bags around my shoulders as Dad started pushing her wheelchair through the hallway. It was a big day at

Asbury, and the nurses and orderlies were lining the hallway and leaning out of the nurses' station to clap for Grandma as we strolled her out. She was like the grand marshal of her own parade. Each congratulatory high five, pat on the back, and enthusiastic shout of encouragement was a reminder of the remarkable resilience she had shown. Members of the care team hugged and squeezed her as she went by. I covered the event like paparazzi, photographing and videoing the whole thing. Grandma just smiled. She was grateful for the love, but not so grateful that she wanted to slow down. She was nudging Dad to get her out of Asbury before anyone changed their minds.

Dad pushed her wheelchair through the automatic exit doors, applied the brake on Grandma's wheelchair, and darted off to get the van, leaving us pining on the curb. Grandma turned to me and said, "Here." She extended her arms and gave me a few folded blankets.

"These are prayer shawls, for the sick and shut-in."

I exclaimed, "But Grandma, you were the one that was sick and shut-in!"

Fairhaven has a prayer shawl ministry where people will knit or crochet shawls or blankets with specific people in mind from beginning to end. And when someone wears the shawl, they have a tangible reminder of the love being directed toward them. Apparently, Grandma had been crocheting prayer shawls for the sick and shut-in the entire time she was sick and shut-in.

I looked at the stack of shawls she'd made—soft, warm, and full of intention. Even in her suffering, she had been thinking of others. I shouldn't have been surprised. This is after all the same woman who views insomnia as an opportunity to pray for others. Always giving.

I told her of course I would deliver them.

Our moment was interrupted by a nurse who had missed Grandma's departure parade and wanted to take a picture with the famous "Ms. Pearl." Grandma smiled big for the selfie.

"You take care now, you hear?" Grandma encouraged the nurse.

When I left the White House, I had prepared myself to spend precious moments with Grandma during what I feared would be her final days. I felt it was my duty to hold her hand the same way I'd watched her hold so many people's hands when I was a kid. I wanted to offer her the same gifts of dignity I'd seen her offer others.

Our time together had always been hopeful and full of meaning and laughter, but there was always a cloud of somberness, however distant, of bidding her the long farewell. But now, unexpectedly, there was joy. Defying all expectations, except her own, Grandma was going home.

Dad pulled the car around and we took her to her favorite restaurant: IHOP.

19

NOT LONG AFTER WE GOT GRANDMA SITUATED AT HOME, I got a call from Dr. Melissa Blair asking to meet with me and Pastor Esther Holimon. At the time, I thought that it was about a grant or an update on some student research. Dr. Blair, the UMBC history professor, had become a friend and trusted advisor on our project. Her students had been doing important work at Pleasant View, researching the history of the buildings, identifying burial records, and compiling an application to place Pleasant View on the National Register of Historic Places.

I don't know what it is about historians requesting an audience, but like Tony Cohen, Dr. Blair asked to meet with me and Pastor Holimon, the relatively new pastor at Fairhaven. We always chuckled because her name was so close to Aunt Esther's maiden name—Esther Hallman (even closer when you say them out loud). Pastor Holimon was the first female pastor appointed at Fairhaven. I don't recall anyone making a big deal about it, but I took it to be a continued intention to try to reflect the diversity of the congregation. Fairhaven had hosted white, Black, and Asian pastors before, all men—Pastor Holimon, a Black woman, added a new dimension of diversity and perspective to the church congregation.

We gathered at Fairhaven during the pastor's office hours and pulled a few folding chairs into a semicircle at the front of the sanctuary, in the very spot where Rev. Glenn Young baptized me as a newborn and I had rung handbells in the youth choir. Pastor Holimon shot a look at me as if to say, *What did you get me into?*

Dr. Blair came armed with documents and folders, a rolled-up map, and the energy of someone who had just unlocked a puzzle piece. She shared her first document, an aerial view printout from Google Maps. We hovered over it, pointing out familiar landmarks: Riffle Ford Road, the house where the Howards had lived, Fairhaven, the edge of the property where my grandma and her siblings had grown up.

Dr. Blair then pulled out the 1865 Martenet and Bond's map of Montgomery County. I had seen this map before. It was created by surveyor Simon Martenet and businessman Thomas Bond; the maps were a post–Civil War snapshot to locate landownership and document economic and social activity. It was so fascinating to go back in time and connect names to places. But the map didn't capture the existence of many of the Black homeowners in the area.

I pointed out Nathan Jones's farm on the map. Jones Lane is now a well-known neighborhood thoroughfare in the community, and Kisha, Maya, and I all went to Jones Lane Elementary School. I had spent kindergarten at Travilah, as Jones Lane didn't yet exist. But Dr. Blair didn't bring us here so that I could trace the lineage of my elementary school. I handed the 1865 map back to her. Pastor Holimon and I waited for Dr. Blair to reveal why we were gathered.

"We have been doing some research. And it appears that Fairhaven sits on the land that was once part of Albert Cissel's farm."

I recognized that name. Grandma had talked about Cissel's farm growing up. It was the big farm next to their homeplace. Grandma and her siblings would play in their fields, and if they needed extra money they would look for farmwork at the Cissel place.

Dr. Blair affirmed this. "According to a 1955 *Montgomery Sentinel* article, this"—she pointed to the farm on the map— "was a working dairy farm with at least ninety head of cattle that had been in the Cissel family since 1898."

Hearing that and then having it confirmed in the records felt like being in Israel and visiting a place that had been the subject of Bible stories; suddenly it became tangible. Grandma's memories of the Cissel farm now had a date, a place, and a map. I was grateful to Dr. Blair for making the connection. But she wasn't done.

"We started pulling land records and going even further back in time," Dr. Blair continued, her voice rising with a mix of reverence and excitement. "And we kept going back in time, and we were able to trace this land where Fairhaven now sits back. It was once part of a much larger farm. As we got back into the nineteenth century and even prior to the Civil War, we learned that this farm was owned by Samuel and Eliza Higgins."

The name hit me all at once. I froze.

Dr. Blair marshaled on, "The Higgins owned Matilda Green and her children. This is the farm where Matilda lived. Where she toiled. Where she attempted to carve out a life as an enslaved person. And all that happened not at some random place. That literally happened *here*."

I couldn't speak.

I stared at the map, trying to process what I was hearing. This land? This sanctuary? These pews? I whispered, "Here?"

It wasn't just that my great-great-grandmother had been enslaved. It was that she had *lived* here. Walked this land. Made a life on it. Breathed here. Endured here. This wasn't some distant, faceless place; it was home.

My mind drifted back to Grandma and her childhood stories of playing at Cissel's farm, running over land that had once enslaved our family. She may have even worked that land not knowing the story beneath her own feet. That was the most confounding part: The ascent from slavery to freedom had happened literally next door, and yet it was never spoken of.

Dr. Blair layered the aerial Google map over the 1865 map; they overlapped perfectly.

We stepped outside as if we might find something in the earth, an artifact or some trace. Lost among the branches, roots, and my own thoughts, but still within the shadow of the steeple, I thought about what this could possibly mean. Perhaps some of the trees right before me had provided shade or sanctuary for my ancestors.

I glided my hand along the old fence posts and wondered

if Matilda had ever done the same. Had she ever walked this exact stretch? I felt connected to my people.

And while Dr. Blair kept talking, excitedly, honored by the discovery, still very much the scholar, I felt my heart sink.

I realized how much I hadn't asked.

I had been preparing myself for a slavery story. I expected something like Montgomery, Alabama, but didn't expect it to be Montgomery County, Maryland. That discovery alone had once felt enormous. But I'd stopped there. *Why?*

The truth had literally been right beneath our feet this entire time. I'd grown up at Fairhaven. Roamed the grounds. Played on it. Worshipped on it. But I never knew that it held this kind of memory. The earlier reveal had made slavery feel close generationally, but this made it feel proximate. It made it real and personal.

Pastor Holimon began to reflect Dr. Blair's enthusiasm over the revelation, weaving in her own thoughts on the redemptive process. "Depending upon the lens through which one views the world," she shared, "in every person, every activity, and every deed, we can find purpose."

I remembered the sermon she had preached on purpose but struggled to find purpose in the fact that my ancestors had been enslaved.

"There is no purpose in this," I muttered.

Pastor Holimon turned to meet my eyes. "Certainly not in the suffering but maybe in what was built after. Maybe in what we are still building."

As I struggled with the purpose, I did reflect on the near impossibility of it all. It felt providential. Fairhaven now stood on the land where that enslavement had taken place.

I had long thought it fateful that the Pleasant View meeting to discuss the church merger took place the same night that Dr. King was assassinated.

I mean, what were the chances?

What were the chances that descendants of both enslaved and enslaver would one day build a church together?

That the very land that once enslaved my family would become the ground where their descendants would build a sanctuary.

It seems so improbable when you put it down on paper. That it happened unknowingly, just by trying, stumbling, and praying their way toward something better. It feels like history folding back on itself in some weird symmetry.

And what I had to remind myself was that this wasn't just history to be studied.

It was our story that we were still putting together one piece at a time.

20

A FEW WEEKS AFTER DAD BROUGHT GRANDMA HOME FROM Asbury, we met at her house to demo her bathroom, which now had to accommodate her wheelchair. Kisha joined us and we wielded sledgehammers and showed off skills Kisha, Maya, and I had all learned as teens attending the Christian Appalachian Missions Project Joining Other Youth (CAMP JOY)—a summer mission project in West Virginia and western Maryland where we'd replace old ramps, build additions, and install running water for those in need.

Grandma interrupted with a question. "Do you all think I could make it to Bible study this evening?" We all looked at one another. Before we could even respond, she answered her own question. "Oh shoot. I can't see. I can't hear. Don't know what I'd go for anyway." And she broke out laughing at her own joke.

It was so good to see her smiling. She had faced more than her share of adversity. Despite all the hardship, I marveled at how Grandma never seemed to lose her faith or her sense of humor. If ever asked the secret to long life, she'd say, "Keep on living!"

Kisha used the interruption to rush back to work, while I joined Dad for the quarter-mile stretch from Grandma's house back to Mom and Dad's at the base of Fellowship Lane.

I spent most of my life observing my father. Growing up, I'd wanted to be just like him. I'd even contemplated following him into the ministry until he counseled me to pursue my own path. I'd read the books on his shelf. Mastered most of his movements and could almost—almost—mimic his sermon delivery.

Dad has this long stride that hinges at the hip more than the knee. I'd practiced it. It looked confident, like he knew this place and was comfortable being from here. Just like when he used to deftly navigate those potholes when we were kids, he knew his way around.

I had noticed him making slight nods along our walk, acknowledging things were in their place. It reminded me of the quiet assurance he always seemed to carry when I used to tag along with him to work, or on our special Chinese food or Jerry's Subs lunches, or even when I'd be sitting beside him at the barbershop and would catch him nod to another Black man.

"Did you know that man, Dad?" I would ask, pulling on his arm and pointing back to the man from the secret cult I was sure my father was a part of.

"No, son, I didn't know him."

"Well, why did you nod hello?"

"You'll understand someday."

That's all he would say. I'm not sure if he didn't want to explain it, or if he just didn't know exactly how to explain the Black man head nod to a five-year-old.

I was real aggressive with it at first, just staring Black men in the face and then giving them a pronounced head nod when they finally made eye contact. It took circumstance to understand that the Black man head nod is a necessity. The head nod is rooted in the need to create safe spaces. When Black men see each other, the head nod is one of acknowledgment. Affirmation. It is a way of saying "I see you," not just socially but in a sea of potentially unfriendly people in an unwelcome land. And, should something happen, I've got your back. A secret society rooted in survival.

As we walked, I couldn't help but think about what I'd just learned at Fairhaven. It changed how I saw everything around us: the soil, the road, the houses. I was searching for traces of the past.

Dad and I walked past some of the new houses that were constructed on the land that was once owned by my grandmother and her siblings, and my father offered, "You know, it just was a lot safer back when you knew your neighbors."

I did a double take when that phrase tumbled out of my father's mouth, particularly as we leisurely strolled down the sidewalk.

First, by every conceivable measure, what Dad said was factually inaccurate. Crime in the community was virtually nonexistent. And by that point I'd done enough archival newspaper searches on Quince Orchard to know that back in the day it had its fair share of thefts, shootings, and even an abduction for ransom. Hell, let's not forget that poor Donald Snyder, the owner of the only general store, was shot in the head right in the center of town! So, it was a bit of a stretch to say that the community was safer *back then*. But Dad was expressing something else. There was a lot wrapped up in that statement, but very little of it had to do with safety.

And second, Dad had made *knowing* people his life's work.

Dad pointed toward two huge houses that had been developed where Ms. Dyson's little one-story rambler had once stood. A fenced-in mega mansion with an iron fence now occupied the footprint of Ms. Talley's house and her pink concrete garage. And Hallman Grove was now a development on the thirteen acres of land at the end of our street. There was so much new development, and we bemoaned each new house.

Grandpa Green had built several homes throughout the community, including three on our street. He would gift the homes to young couples with budding families as a foundation for the future. Over time, two of those homes had been replaced with newer builds by the next generation of those families. No one protested when the Thompson or Greene children tore down and rebuilt on their lot, or even when my sister Kisha purchased Grandpa's old pig farm to build her home.

Perhaps it's because we knew them. They were one of *us*, and we give each other the benefit of the doubt.

Though the construction of the new houses in town was a painful reminder of the loss, the issue was really with the people. "Things were safer when you knew your neighbors" was my father's way of expressing frustration about the aggressive amount of change happening throughout the community and the disconnect with the new people change had brought.

Quince Orchard had been a small community where it was easy to know your neighbors—most of which were family. Folks went to church together. For generations, children went to the one school in town. When the snow came, your neighbors helped shovel you out. Neighbors were each other's insurance policy. They would check in on one another and share a meal together. When the community is interconnected, it can develop a value system. Trust and accountability start between people and then grow to organizations and institutions.

It's always hard when new folk show up, and it becomes harder to build and maintain that social fabric when people don't look like us or talk like us or vote like us or love like us. But that doesn't mean it is any less possible or any less important. Grandma had shown me that through the Quince Orchard and Fairhaven stories. She told me what was possible with incremental steps and hands reaching across the aisles. With a healthy heaping of prayer and intention, we could create community. And not just community for community's sake, but to build the social bonds that allow us to accomplish something meaningful—together.

I turned to my father and put my arm around him. Then I tried to conjure my best Gerry Green counselor voice: "As Grandma once told me, back in 1968, Grandpa disagreed with the proposed church merger, and all y'all voted for it, including you and Grandma. Grandpa Green held out, but nonetheless, Grandma moved forward with her decision, and somehow, she did it with love. She never shut the door and continued to offer Grandpa on-ramps. She seemed to know that we all travel at our own pace."

As we neared the cul-de-sac at the base of Fellowship Lane, I asked, "Do you remember the day that a paved Fellowship Lane was dedicated?"

I wore a bright red-and-brown outfit with calf-high white striped socks to match. It was the '80s and I just knew I looked good.

"Those huge paving trucks had been parked on our street for weeks. But when the day came, everyone showed up. Fairhaven represented. Kisha's Brownie troop carried the colors. I remember Mom running around pregnant with Maya and carrying around a clipboard with to-do tasks on it. Even Ike Leggett, the first Black county councilman, was there. It felt like a real moment."

A dedication for a little lane seems small, but it mattered. That lane connected the people who lived on it to jobs and school, and when heavy rain or snowstorms made it impassable, life was disrupted. And everyone showed up because that's just what we did back then. We showed up for each other and this was a long time coming.

A colorful ribbon stretched across the entire cul-de-sac. Papa Bell, the oldest resident on that lane, Rev. Talley's father, and Grandma's father-in-law from her first marriage, dressed in a stylish cap, sat in a chair at the center. Ike stood beside him, and together they cut the ribbon.

Dad added, "Even the Kinderman was there." The Kinderman was a high-energy emcee that was a staple at the May-Fest celebrations. He was like the Electric Slide personified, who had everyone up and dancing.

"I heard that day almost didn't happen," I added slyly. "The county kept dragging its feet on paving the road. Grandpa got fed up and rallied folks to speak before the County Council, including Rev. Young, the white pastor at Fairhaven."

I relished the opportunity to lecture Dad. "You know that even though Grandpa didn't officially merge, Rev. Young would still call the house, stop by to sit with Grandpa, and if something needed fixing at the church or the lawn needed mowing,

Grandpa's was the call. That slow trust building meant something. And when Grandpa needed support, he leaned on Rev. Young to testify before the County Council. And, as you know, in his own time, Grandpa even became a member of Fairhaven."

I watched Dad wrestle with that truth. He quietly looked around at the land his family had once owned and the street he had helped pave. The land his mother was sued over. The same land where the developer placed a house directly across the street from my parents'—adding insult to injury.

The frustration over the development was often aimed at the new arrivals—people who didn't know what had happened here.

My father turned to me and asked, almost to himself, "But how could they know? If they just got here, how could they know the history of this community? How could they know the good that happened here? And even some of the heartache."

To my surprise he added, "Maybe it's the responsibility of those who know the history and want to preserve it to share that history with those who don't know."

The very next day, wrapped in my robe, I watched my parents out of their front window as they carried a new plant to welcome the Asian family that had moved into that house across the street. My heart swelled. This felt like a rededication to the principles of community. It was real-life action. A small but meaningful step in the right direction.

For a kid like me who grew up on the promises of the Beloved Community, raised to believe that shared spaces could lead to shared understanding, this gesture meant everything.

Until May 25, 2020.

21

For nine minutes and twenty-nine seconds, a Minneapolis police officer held his knee on the neck of Mr. George Floyd, a Black man detained for suspicion of passing a counterfeit $20 bill. The haunting moment was captured on video by a teenage bystander, and as Mr. Floyd repeatedly pleaded that he couldn't breathe, he called out for his dead mother. The entire world bore witness to his tragic fate.

Of course, Mr. Floyd wasn't the first or last. Just two months earlier, on March 13, 2020, Ms. Breonna Taylor, a twenty-six-year-old emergency medical technician, had been shot and killed in her home during a no-knock warrant by Louisville Metro Police officers. Weeks before that, on February 23, 2020, Mr. Ahmaud Arbery, a twenty-five-year-old Black man, was chased and fatally shot while jogging in Glynn County, Georgia, by armed residents. Their names joined a growing, anguished roll call: Mr. Freddie Gray, whose spine was shattered in the back of a Baltimore police van. Mr. Trayvon Martin, a teenager walking home from a convenience store with Skittles and a can of Sprite. Not every name made national news. Not every loss was filmed. But this felt like a tipping point that had been welling for centuries.

The brutality against Mr. Floyd unfolded before an undistracted global gaze and triggered a massive response. Because of the Covid-19 pandemic, the world had finally slowed down. And in that stillness, the country could not ignore the treatment of Mr. Floyd. *I* finally slowed down and took notice. Every unarmed Black death had cracked something in me. But I had kept moving, busying myself as if the busyness would make everything okay. As if that might be an escape from the reality of being Black in America.

As Derek Chauvin's knee snuffed the life out of Mr. Floyd, I felt my hope for humanity begin to extinguish. I had just been preaching at my father about allyship and against the us-versus-them mentality. Yet, suddenly, it felt like the story I'd been told, and had begun telling, was fake.

I had been fed a dream of a community where justice might flow like water and righteousness like a mighty stream, only to discover from empty bucket after empty bucket that the well was dry. The hope and aspiration of the Quince Orchard community remained unfulfilled. Unfulfilled—that was all that was real.

The world watched George Floyd die. It wasn't new. It was just finally caught on camera. Maybe that's what Quince Orchard had been trying to tell me. That neglect and erasure is a kind of violence too. When we fail to preserve memory, when we ignore the names and the land and the legacy, we let lives slip away without witness.

Mr. Floyd's murder was a rupture. But the fracture wasn't sudden. It had been spreading beneath us for generations. I just hadn't wanted to see it. Not in my country. Not in myself.

And it wasn't just the interracial, intergenerational utopia of Fairhaven that was suddenly exposed to me as a mirage. Dean McLeod's vision of being known by name and by story collapsed in a country where George Floyd could be killed over a $20 bill. President Obama's post-partisan campaign, envisioning a united nation beyond red and blue states, seemed out of touch in a country where a refusal to acknowledge the ghosts of our past was now the horror of our present. How had I been so naïve as to continuously exalt the notion of "we" in a country consumed by a legacy of unmitigated racial animus?

I had once imagined my life, successful, modern, thirty-something, Black, as a kind of proof. Proof that it was possible to live in the middle, to find common ground, to be the bridge. I believed navigating the gray areas between sociopolitical extremes, reconciling and extending the first hand, calling everyone back to the table was the work. That the effort itself was the reward.

But that middle ground gave way beneath my feet.

It turned out, if you belonged to all the tribes, you were part of none.

Despite my efforts to hold space for multiple truths, to tolerate and translate, it suddenly felt hollow. And exhausting.

I wept for Mr. Floyd, and I selfishly cried for myself.

Had my whole life simply been a performance? I felt duped.

I felt like a fool because I had believed patience and compromise would lead to justice. Worse, a fraud, because I had preached it. And now I didn't know what was left.

I could taste an anger I'd spent a lifetime suppressing. I was tired of shrinking myself to appear nonthreatening. Tired of whistling on the sidewalk or in the elevator to put white people at ease. Tired of the familiar knots in my stomach every time a cop passed. Exhausted trying to prove by example to anyone looking that Black lives matter.

I was fed up from a lifetime of being asked to offer a perspective for an entire race, yet having my ethnicity questioned because of the color of my eyes, of being confronted with racist questions masquerading as intellectual curiosity. I was simply done being mistaken for other Black men and then being told it's a compliment. Spent from feeling guilty for growing up in a two-parent household as if that somehow wasn't an authentic Black experience. Done with hearing words like wigger—defined as a white person who tries to emulate or acquire cultural behavior and tastes attributed to African Americans—thrown around and that being perfectly alright. Every bone in my body was fatigued by the rush to reconciliation without the work of confronting the truth. *Jesus, how many times had I been guilty of doing the rushing?*

During the span of the summer protests, all the community building, the searching for grace, understanding, and common ground that had previously defined my days felt so insignificant. It all felt too small, too inconsequential, too accommodating, too incremental to combat something so big and powerful, so violent and consuming as unbridled racism and hate. *Why would a nation with so much promise refuse to overcome? Had our collective hurt replaced any notion of collective hope?* I retweeted a post that said: "We're not asking you to kill them like you kill us. Just don't kill us like you don't kill them."

Us. Them.

His murder had stripped away my last layer of belief in we—that fragile creed written into our founding documents.

I sought solace in the shower, the cascading water masking a stream of tears. I didn't have to be strong and exude outward confidence. Alone, I could be pitiful. Naked and afraid.

In the weeks that followed, not even showers could wash away my profound sense of guilt. The recognition of my own privilege in the face of systemic injustice became a new source of self-contempt. I felt bad about feeling bad. I felt pulled under.

In the throes of such despair, I thought about going to see Grandma. I did, I truly did. I thought about just going to sit with her. One day, I'd even put my shoes on, which given my state of mind was a considerable step. I could picture her, sitting in the dining room at the table, poring over her Avon orders with a blanket wrapped over her shoulders. But I already knew exactly what she was going to say. She was going to say something hopeful that I didn't want to hear. Something like, "It takes a long time sometimes, but with faith in God, I believe we will get there." I couldn't go back to that. I was tired of long times. I was tired of blind faith. And I was not convinced we would actually get there.

I flicked my shoes off and found my way back to the couch.

22

THE DAYS BLURRED. 2021 CAME, BUT I BARELY NOTICED. I'd been in different stages of isolation since Mr. Floyd's murder, slipping deeper into it without realizing how far I'd gone. I'd stopped responding to texts from friends. I moved from my communal condo building overlooking the bustling Baltimore Inner Harbor to a one-bedroom basement apartment with a view of a brick garage. I'd tried to write but my words were uninspired. I told my partner that I needed space, I didn't know how much, but I knew I was falling and didn't want to take us down too.

I was angry about his murder—all the murders—and how it had undone my trust in community, in the idea of being known by name and by story, in the belief that we would get over.

Since Election Day, Donald Trump had continued to perpetuate his lie claiming that the 2020 election was stolen from him. On January 6, 2021, I was sitting in my D.C. apartment with my laptop open, attempting to work. I was supposed to be doing my part, but I had retreated and was distant. I'd become a bad business partner too.

CNN was on in the background. Like a commuter rubber-necking to see the crash, I kept glancing up at Trump's "Stop the Steal" rally to see what mess he was stirring up now. Then I saw the White House being used as a political backdrop.

I was already pretty broken by that point, but that just gutted me. I had worked in that building. I had protected its image. I believed in what I thought it represented. Now it was being twisted, used as a prop.

As Lee Greenwood's "God Bless the U.S.A." blared over the crowd and Trump urged his supporters to "fight like hell," I'd had enough.

As my grandmother would say, I got up and "cut it off." The TV. The noise. The theater.

Silence was better.

At 2:48 P.M. I got an imminent extreme alert notification text stating that D.C. mayor Muriel Bowser was implementing a citywide curfew to take effect at 6 P.M. I cut the television back on. As CNN anchors tag-teamed the coverage of a chaotic scene, protestors had breached a police perimeter on the west side of the U.S. Capitol Building. I paced back and forth in my basement apartment in sheer disbelief. I shot off a few "Can you believe this?" texts to former colleagues.

As the protestors morphed into rioters then insurrectionists armed with pipes, bear spray, and other tactical weapons, some broke through barriers, assaulting law-enforcement officers, and swept the chambers looking for lawmakers who were at the Capitol to certify the results of the 2020 election. I was utterly transfixed, watching in disbelief, praying that the violence would dissipate.

I kept pacing.

I had to *do* something. I grabbed my keys and got in my car but talked myself down. The scene at the Capitol was deteriorating, and I couldn't understand why law enforcement hadn't completely shut it down. I nodded at what so many had already texted me: "If they were Black, this thing would've *been* over!"

A friend connected me to a local FOX 5 reporter who was searching for reactions to what was happening at the Capitol. I replied that I didn't think I had anything novel to share. We traded a few texts and scheduled time to talk, but then no call materialized. But the back-and-forth planted the seed even further in my head that I needed to get to the Capitol. I knew that if I was going to go, it needed to be before the curfew. I didn't want to be subject to random stops. Something said: *Go now.* Around 4 P.M., I threw on a hoodie and a jacket and hopped in my car again.

I had no idea exactly why I was going or what I would do, but the impulse to get to the Capitol was reflexive, as if I could somehow make a difference there in person.

And somewhere in that messy impulse to go and bear witness I thought of Grandma. The Grandma who used to take me to volunteer at Asbury when I was a kid. The daily devotional. Her sixty-four years of Avon books. The quiet, consistent presence in places most people avoided. She'd show up. She'd sit. She'd listen. She'd witness.

It wasn't resistance in the way the world labels it, but it was just that. She reminded me that sometimes showing up *was* the work. That presence mattered. That dignity could live in the small things.

I didn't know what I'd find at the Capitol. But I could show up. I could stand in it. I could carry that part of her.

I crossed the John Philip Sousa Bridge over the Anacostia River and drove northwestward up Pennsylvania Avenue. The route was eerily silent and vacant. I kept my head on swivel scanning the deserted streets, a block ahead and over, for signs of unrest. Even the air inside the car felt charged, as if the electricity of the city had somehow seeped in.

I received my tactical updates from that strategic military site, NPR, as anyone intending to foil an insurrection naturally would. NPR offered fragmented updates, yet the urgency of the unfolding events seemed incongruent with the calm cadence of their reporting on a "a city in turmoil." Everything was just surreal.

As soon as I crossed the bridge, I could see the Capitol dome, with the bronze Statue of Freedom perched atop, ahead through barren tree branches. I was prepared to bob and weave through neighborhood side streets, but there was nothing stopping my advance up Pennsylvania Avenue. Twelve blocks. Nine blocks. Five blocks away. Finally, I was halted by a sea of police lights and barricades, but only two officers signaling for me to stop as I got to Pennsylvania and 2nd Avenue SE, just two blocks from the Capitol.

A uniformed officer, stern-faced and authoritative, stepped forward. I rolled down my window, and his voice cut through the mild but breezy January evening.

"Sir, the area is restricted. You cannot proceed any further. Please remain in your vehicle, turn around, and find an alternate route," he instructed. His voice didn't carry any of the urgency I'd expected—no trace of the chaos unfolding just a few blocks away. I looked back in disbelief. Didn't he understand that the Capitol was under siege? That his buddies were under assault? They didn't have this under control!

"I'm here to help," I managed.

The officer repeated a version of the above and pointed me to turn off Pennsylvania Avenue.

I was one of the "good guys" and was there to help, and from what I saw on TV they needed the help! I couldn't understand why the police were there telling me to stop, when every person with a badge and uniform needed to be at the Capitol throwing down.

I got ahold of myself. I wasn't going to be able to stop it. I started to turn the car around. But I still felt an intense urge to step into the evening air. I needed to get out and feel it, and not just drive away. I needed to at least be present in that place, at that moment, without the safety or confines of the car.

I looped back on Pennsylvania Avenue before stopping around 3rd or 4th Street SE. I put the car in park but didn't even turn it off. I didn't plan to stay long. I stepped out of the vehicle. I needed to stand there and be present, to mark what was happening with my own eyes, for myself and those who couldn't. I walked into the middle of a deserted Pennsylvania Avenue. The Capitol dome protruded into the evening sky. I had taken one last mental snapshot of the scene when I noticed a man on the sidewalk draped in Trump gear. Still drunk with rebellion, as he crossed my path he stopped and turned to look in my direction. I saw his face and he saw mine. He couldn't have been more than twenty feet away.

One Saturday morning, when my sister Kisha and I were about eight and five, respectively, Maya wasn't even born yet, our cartoons spree was interrupted by a door slam and raised voices in the kitchen, which were both rare. We crept to the top of the split-level stairs and could hear Mom and Dad. The kitchen radio, which played nonstop in our house, had been turned off, so we knew this was serious.

Mom and Dad spoke in hushed tones, but we could still hear. Surprised they didn't take it to their room. Dad's voice rose and fell as he recounted what had happened to him. Not like when he was in the pulpit. This sounded more emotional. Less rehearsed, less in control.

Dad had been jogging north on Route 28 toward Darnestown. Shortly after he passed Fairhaven Church on his right and Jones Lane on his left, a pickup truck was coming up behind him. In my mind it's always red, though I can't recall if he ever said that. As the truck got closer to him, someone leaned out of the passenger's window. Dad felt their presence pushing him off the road, forcing him from the shoulder into the grass. As they passed him, they hurled a "Nigger, go home!" in his direction and sped off.

For the past three decades, whenever I've revisited that memory, I can hear the laughter of the man in the pickup truck, callous and indifferent to the hurt he caused my father. I can envision his worn and wrinkled face. The face I had imagined for years was the face of the man staring me down on Pennsylvania Avenue.

Unlike him, I wore no identifying clothes, no campaign buttons or stickers, nothing to suggest who my guy was in the 2020 election. The only identifier I was wearing that evening was the one that I cannot remove. Looking dead at me, he yelled, "You're gonna die!"

His aggression caught me off guard. I looked over both shoulders and I was still the only other person standing on the street. *Was this dude yelling at me?* The cops' attention was rightly on the Capitol Building. An empty Metro bus, a few blocks away, pulled off in the opposite direction. I was alone.

I turned back to the man. *Was he about to come at me?* I could feel the hair on the back of my neck stand up, my heart beginning to pound. The surge of adrenaline had a primal effect. An unsteady energy coursed through me, in preparation for whatever might come next. Again, louder this time, he hurled, "You're gonna die!" Then, as if proclaiming the executioner, he yelled, "TRUMP!"

I just stood there. On a street corner in our nation's capital.

God, for an instant it felt like I was back on Fellowship Lane, frozen in place, being heckled with chants of *"You don't belong here!"*

I was being told I didn't belong all over again.

Not here.

Not there.

Not on this earth.

That my life not only could be taken but would be.

Back on Fellowship Lane, I didn't get angry with that kid despite his hurling racial slurs. This time, I was done holding it all in. If this guy wanted it, I was going to give him all the suppressed rage my body held. The kind that shakes your ribs from the inside. One of us wasn't going to walk away. I watched him closely. I wasn't the same kid anymore. I was a grown man, coiled so tight by years of being good, hopeful, affable, I was ready to snap.

He stepped even closer. We circled each other, trying to figure out who would make the first move.

One more step, I told myself. *One more step, and I'll break his neck.*

In a flash, the whole scene played out in my mind—an act of self-defense where I would finally assert my right, my father's right, all of our right, to exist without terror, to be unafraid, and to belong wherever I am just because I am.

But another vision flashed through my mind too. The police. Guns drawn. Voices shouting, *Stop!* My body incapable or unwilling, and a headline being written: "I told him to stay in the vehicle."

Even if I won that moment, I didn't think I'd survive what would come after. Even in my rage I had to be constrained.

I unclenched my hands as I started to back away. His threats got even louder. Bolder. But now I could hear the performance in his voice. He wasn't going to do shit. He needed someone to play the part he'd already cast. But I'd made my decision.

I moved toward my car, which was now between us. When I opened the door and stepped inside, he started to back off, still shouting, lumbering farther down Pennsylvania Avenue toward Barracks Row.

I sat there for a moment, my whole body a ball of adrenaline. I was shaking. It had taken every ounce of restraint in my body to hold me back. At some point, I gently pressed the gas and eased the car away. I didn't know where I was going. I wasn't ready to talk. I couldn't sit still. So, I drove.

There were more police headlights up the road on Pennsylvania Avenue, so I veered onto 3rd Street and merged onto 395 South.

I couldn't take the silence as I merged onto a desolate

George Washington Parkway, which was probably a good thing because I think I was only going like five miles per hour. Everyone must have been home glued to the news. I didn't want to hear another word about the Capitol. So, I searched for music to break the silence.

I cycled through the preprogrammed radio stations until I landed on a station playing "Stand."

I belted along verse after verse because I wanted to believe it. *After you've done all you can . . . you just stand.*

As the song faded into the background, the moment flashed back. I played it over and over in my mind. He had decided I was on the other team and that was enough to make me expendable. *How is that even possible?* I wondered what face he conjured when he looked at me.

The car sort of navigated itself, and before I knew it I was back in Quince Orchard. By the time I got there, the light in Grandma's front room was already off. I didn't want to disturb her. Without anywhere else to go, I drifted onto Cousin Melvin's old running route. The town was familiar, and at the same time foreign. Some homes were gone. Others, newly built. I passed my parents' house without stopping. I wasn't ready to explain where I'd been or what had almost happened.

I wasn't ready to go home yet. Driving around alone felt better than being in my apartment alone. Eventually, I pulled onto the same loose gravel that Melvin and I had jogged. The gravel that had announced the arrival of those pioneers on the evening of April 4, 1968. I worked the car into a parking spot near the old church building.

I made my way across the parking lot to the schoolhouse. It was locked. I slid my dad's expired Costco card into the door and picked my way inside. I was a latchkey kid in the '80s and had picked the lock a few times to get into the house when I'd forgotten the key. This, however, was my first time doing so to enter a 150-year-old building. Moonlight streamed through the aging windows, casting long shadows across the floorboards.

The site was looking a bit worse for wear. The wallboards had started to bow, and in some places you could see straight through to the outside. Across the lot, I could see the church also looked fragile and tired. The front was beginning to separate, and the bell tower sagged as if a hard wind might bring it down.

I swept my phone's flashlight across the room and saw the little desks and the potbelly stove. I thought about how Uncle Thompkins would describe being strategic about when he would arrive to school. He didn't want to show up too early and be responsible for carrying the logs and making the fire in the potbelly stove, but if he showed up too late, he would have to clean it out. It's interesting how memories sort of get stored in rooms, waiting to be uncovered.

I saw a frame leaning against the wall behind the stove and crouched closer for a better view. I'd seen the plaque before but had never taken the time to really look at it. It was the charter establishing the Pleasant View Methodist Group. At the bottom were the signatures of some of the elders that I'd grown up revering. These were the same men that would come and dig out the snowy cars on Fellowship Lane and pitch horseshoes late into the night with Grandpa Green. They were the women who had led Sunday School, taught us to wrap the maypole, and made sure we didn't misbehave.

Their signatures were etched with intention on the charter,

from a time when a signature meant something, just below, in big, bold block letters—PLEASANT VIEW METHODIST CHURCH IN QUINCE ORCHARD, MARYLAND. Pleasant View had been witness to Quince Orchard's rise and fade, joys and reckonings.

Then I noticed for the first time the words inscribed at the top of the document. Like the stories Grandma told, they hadn't revealed themselves to me all at once, waiting, apparently, until I was ready to receive them. There, centered neatly in a ribbon border, were words from James 1:22:

BE YE DOERS OF THE WORD, AND NOT HEARERS ONLY

There it was. My grandmother's simple yet profound manifesto—doers do. *It was from the Bible.*

I looked out the window at the cascade of tombstones against the night sky. One hundred fifty years of ancestry, of history, of receipts laid out before me. A field of defiant names with impossible dreams. They had believed in something better, even when everything around them tried to tell them otherwise. I felt naïve for believing too much, and for a moment even questioned whether their dreams had been foolish too.

For a long time, I'd kept anger at a distance. I told myself it wasn't productive. But the truth is I think I was afraid that if I truly embraced and gave voice to the anger, I'd betray the respectability I'd learned to prize. The poise, patience, and civility.

But now I couldn't just put it down. Not without putting down a part of me.

As I looked out the window across that legacy of hope, I wondered if those who had come before me had been angry too. *How could they not have been?*

Gary and Matilda, my great-great-grandparents, endured the indignity and injustice of slavery. They were not anomalies. They were part of a generation of Black people who stood resilient in the wake of emancipation's broken promises. They didn't have the luxury of time for revenge seeking. They were busy building schools and fortifying communities, worlds rooted in dignity and wholly sustained by a vision for generations they would never meet. Something freer than what they had inherited.

Grandma Green had been run off from job interviews, relegated to domestic labor, ridiculed for asking for a moderate raise, and she watched her children attend segregated schools. I suspect she was angry. She used it. She Sunday Schooled that anger. She merged churches with that anger. She put children through college with that anger.

I began to understand that my ancestors hadn't built this place by hiding their pain but by using it to transform their world. Confusion or frustration or setback hadn't shut them down. They folded it into labor and love and structures that could hold both grief and possibility. Surrounded by the quiet of that dark, dilapidated room, I didn't have to imagine their presence. I could see the results of their impassioned work. The structure was strained but still holding.

That's how I felt too.

I had stepped into the schoolhouse feeling like a fraud, unsure if the outrage swelling in me was a betrayal or a breakthrough. I'd spent so long reaching for the middle, thinking moderation was where progress lived. But the longer I stood there and let myself feel, the more pieces started to shift.

I remembered how during our argument Uncle Vernon

had yelled, "It's down there," pointing in Pleasant View's direction. Back then, I thought he was just referring to two old buildings and a cemetery plot. But now I think he was naming something else—our inheritance. For most of my life, I had thought that meant grace. The gift of faith. But what I'd inherited, at its core, was a many-generations-long freedom struggle.

That evening, I'd wandered into the old schoolhouse dazed and looking for a place to put my frustration. I found a space for all of it. I could see what was truly at risk. It wasn't just the land. Or the church or the schoolhouse. Or even the stories. It was the belief, the tenuous, tenacious belief that despite hate and hardship, they—we—might build something better.

The rage had made me selfish. Jaded. Skeptical of people and even more suspicious of purpose. I had pulled back and stopped reaching.

People sometimes talk about what's been lost. As if we have no role to play. But the greater concern is what we fail to hold on to. The rituals that shaped us. The places that orient us. The values we were taught before we could even name them.

I realized that what the people of Quince Orchard left behind in Pleasant View wasn't a relic or an ending. They bequeathed another example of the Black communal tradition of taking action in the face of impossible odds while holding fast to the possibility of something better: A place to seek sanctuary. A place to learn. A place to focus our anger. A place to commune. A place to dream. A place to build. A place to restore. A place to remember.

A place to begin again.

EPILOGUE

Spring 2025

W E HAD BEEN PLANNING A CELEBRATION TO REOPEN the Pleasant View site. I can clearly see Grandma in her wheelchair, still going at 106, critically eyeing the plans.

For years, the Pleasant View Historical Association had worked to save what those generations that came before us had built. We'd raised funds, applied for historic preservation grants, and rallied the community to rebuild the foundation of the schoolhouse and shore up the century-old beams of the church that had stood as a beacon since the 1800s.

When we gathered next as a community, it was the kind of day you'd hope for, not a cloud in the endless blue canvas above Quince Orchard. Perfect for a day of remembrance. But our plans had to change. Before we could celebrate the restored schoolhouse, the church's new bell tower, or the brick pavers, we first gathered to celebrate and honor a life well lived.

It had been just over a week since my son's early morning appointment at the pediatrician's office. Since Kisha's call. Since "It's her foot again" preceded the words more final than I was prepared for: "Grandma has passed." She was just two months shy of her 107th birthday.

We gathered first at Fairhaven. The combined choir, of which Grandma had been a member, sang beautifully. Everyone was packed into that little sanctuary, with some overflowing into the fellowship hall—Aunt Esther and Uncle Curt, Uncle Thompkins and Aunt Roberta, in from Tennessee. Uncle Vernon, Uncle Howard, and Aunt Jackie were there, and, of course, Mom and Dad, Kisha and Maya, and all the cousins, Kevin, Tim, Melvin, Sherry, Carolyn, Charles, David, Pam, Darlene, and many more. Dad delivered a powerful eulogy. Uncle Vernon sang a beautiful solo version of "May the Work I've Done Speak for Me," and Uncle Howard wrote a song that all three brothers performed. It was good to have everyone together.

Proclamations came from far and wide, dignitaries lifting up her memory. After a moving service, a procession of cars made its way through the community, passing landmarks that told her story. We passed the old homeplace off Riffle Ford Road. We continued past Quince Orchard High School, for which Grandma, Ms. Ada Howard, Ms. Ridgley, and others had come together to fight for a name that preserved a community's history. As we crawled past the intersection where Donald Snyder's store once stood, I remembered the stories of penny candy and egg trading, tales of a rare place where Black and white residents' paths crossed in segregated Quince Orchard. The cars moved slowly, deliberately, like a stream winding its way home, finally turning onto the gravel path leading to Pleasant View. Back where it all began.

The Pleasant View Methodist Church came into view first, its new steeple sturdy against the sky. Just beyond it, off to the right, stood the Quince Orchard Colored School, where Grandma had started her lessons a century earlier. You could see the care in every corner. The new roof. A solid foundation. An addition off to the side, replacing a portion that had been lost to fire. It looked built to last. The type of work you do when the story isn't over.

People filed out of their vehicles and gathered near Gary and Matilda's tombstone. I donned the white pallbearer gloves they'd given us and positioned myself in formation beside the older cousins I'd looked up to all my life. Together, we carried Grandma to the spot she had picked out, next to our grandfather. Dad stood before us, Bible clutched. The cemetery stretched behind him, headstones marking more than 150 years of ancestors who had helped found this place just four years after emancipation. Each a chapter in a story of resilience, determination, and hope.

WHEN I HAD STEPPED BACK into the room after Kisha broke the news, I looked at my son, Aidan, contentedly playing in Ritu's lap, unaware of how the world had just shifted. I leaned in and whispered to him, "Grandma Green lives on in you now." He cooed back at me, his eyes bright and searching. Understanding what I meant, Ritu's eyes began to well up.

Grandma had a way of seeing things before the rest of us. Whenever she would ask about Aidan, whether with me or with my mom, she would pause and ask, "Spell his name for me, again?"

As Aidan squirmed, something drew my attention to his little blanket wrapped around him with his name embroidered in blue. For the first time, on the very day that she passed, I saw what Grandma may have been trying to tell us all along. Right there staring back at me was her name in his: A-**I-D-A**-N. Without realizing it, I had been guarding Grandma's presence within his name all this time. Like so much of her wisdom, unrevealed until its proper season.

STANDING IN THE CEMETERY AT Pleasant View, Mom began to hum, and then others joined in, voices rising in an impromptu rendition of "Amazing Grace," Grandma's most beloved hymn. Surrounded by the historic buildings, the generations resting beneath the soil, and the layered inheritance now my duty to pass on, the notes of the old hymn seemed to connect the dots that had been guiding my feet for more than a decade, since I took that leap of faith and left the White House to sit by my grandmother's side.

I unfolded the pink funeral program, Grandma's favorite color. *Ida Pearl Green* was printed across the bottom in elegant type. I thought about all the times when I was a little boy and she would lovingly guide my hand, pointing to the words in a hymn so that I could follow along. And just like she taught me, I traced the letters I-D-A with my finger.

ACKNOWLEDGMENTS

To Gary and Matilda, and to all the ancestors whose names we may not know but whose strength we try to carry, thank you for making a way when there was none.

To my grandparents, I love each of you and miss you all dearly. Gerard and Ida Pearl Green, Grandpa and Grandma Green, your lessons, your strengths, and your shortcomings continue to guide me. And to my mother's parents, Earl and Evelyn Harris, PawPaw and MawMaw, who don't get much airtime in this book, thank you for playing an equally important role in raising us to love our neighbors as we love ourselves.

To my parents, you showed me what love in motion looks like and taught me everything I know about faith, humor, grace, and perseverance. I won the lottery with you and am so lucky that I am you.

To my sisters, Maya and Kisha, thank you for standing with me always. Maya, I know these pages focus largely on stories from before you were old enough to be part of them and then while you were busy at medical school making us all proud, but you are no less a central part of who I am and where we come from. And Kisha, my partner in trouble from day one, thank you for co-producing *Finding Fellowship* with me and for all your work in collecting and sharing these stories.

To our extended family, thank you for your willingness to tell our story and to sit with the difficult parts of it. And for showing me how to come back to the table. To the larger Fellowship Lane and Quince Orchard family, thank you for the foundation of memory, faith, and fellowship that you built. You demonstrated what it means to belong to something greater than yourself.

Thank you to the trustees of the Pleasant View Historical Association. Your dedication, selflessness, and stewardship are just extraordinary. This project had a place to begin because of your work and, in particular, that of Vernon Green and Carroll Greene, and the current chairperson and treasurer, Gerard Green, Jr., and Melvin Joppy, Jr., who have worked diligently to collect, preserve, and curate the Black experience in Quince Orchard. To all who have donated their time, talent, and treasure, including the tremendous research from Diane Canova and Mary Cather, to sustain the work and to share the Pleasant View story, thank you!

To my Fairhaven family, thank you for upholding your baptismal covenant to watch over me and for allowing me to put you on display, for trusting me to tell a portion of your story, and to all the pastors who welcomed us into your services even when we were a distraction.

Thank you to everyone who agreed to sit down with me. Your stories gave context and texture to these pages, even if your name does not appear. Once I started this project, some-one asked me what was so special about my family. I told them nothing, and everything. I hope this book gives others license to explore their family and their community and to share the light. I believe that there is power in the everyday stories of regular people putting their heads down to accomplish extraor-dinary things. I hope we can inspire each other.

To the intrepid friends who read an earlier version of this book, Rob Cacace, Cindy Chang, Jamie McIntyre, and Diana Noyes, thank you, your prompting kept me going when the road felt endless. To the friends and family who read this version, Emma Andersson, Logan Beirne, Kisha Davis, Seth Godin, Megan Hogan, Jesse Moore, Sujeet Rao, and Courtney Sieloff, thank you, your insightful, thoughtful feedback sharpened and strengthened the story and pushed me further than I would have otherwise gone.

I'm deeply grateful to Cindy Chang, Joanny Estrella, Char-lie Galbraith, Sujeet Rao, and Rishi Sahgal, who lent me cars, couches, and recording equipment along the way. You literally kept this project moving.

I'm deeply grateful to my editor, Kierna Mayo, and Hiab Debessai and the entire team at One World, whose care and insight guided this book to its final form. And to my agents at Park, Fine and Brower, Mia Vitale and Sarah Passick, thank you for believing in this project from the very beginning and shepherding it with force. To Babette Perry, thank you for being the consummate visionary and connector. To Jim Gilio, my dear friend, thank you for your sage counsel and as always for your friendship.

To members of the Quince Orchard Project, in particular our creative director and dear friend, Dr. Imani Cheers, the classes of students from Quince Orchard High School, American University, Georgetown University, and UMBC who worked to help collect these stories, I'm deeply indebted and amazed at all that you accomplished. A special thank-you to Dr. Sonya Douglass, Dr. Cheryl LaRoche, Tony Cohen, and Dr. Melissa Blair for their groundbreaking work and support. And Matt Logan and the team at Montgomery History for their outstanding research and dedication to preserving history. Thank you to Sarah Rogers and Heritage Montgomery for your commitment to local history and culture.

I also want to thank Robert Raben, who first encouraged me to visit the stations of my grandmother's cross; Donald Graham, who was confident that this was a story worth pursuing; Rick Berndt, who shared that belief and has become a champion of it; and Kathy Ruemmler, who made it all possible.

Finally, to Ritu and Aidan, you changed everything. You are my heart and my home and a testament to all that is too precious to lose.

ABOUT THE AUTHOR

JASON G. GREEN is a Maryland-born community organizer, attorney, storyteller, and entrepreneur. Green served as special assistant to the president and associate White House counsel to President Obama, advising on economic and domestic policy matters. Green co-founded SkillSmart, a pioneering company that reshapes how communities measure economic impact, and is CEO of EverGreen Labs, where he supports a host of visionary organizations working to build trust, expand economic opportunity, and strengthen community.

Green also serves as a trustee to the Pleasant View Historic Association and supports its fundraising campaign to preserve the historic site, and he sits on several advisory boards focused on opportunity and innovation. He is a founding commissioner and former chair of the Montgomery County Commission on Remembrance and Reconciliation. His award-winning documentary, *Finding Fellowship*, available on PBS, explores the rich history of Quince Orchard and the fight to preserve its legacy.

A graduate of Washington University in St. Louis and Yale Law School, Green remains rooted in the work of truth and justice, investing in stories that remind us who we are. He splits his time between Maryland and Dallas, Texas, with his wife, Ritu, and son, Aidan.

tooprecioustolose.com